Syd Field

Author of the critically applauded

Screenplay

"Full of common sense, an uncommon commodity."
—*Esquire*
"Quite simply the only manual to be taken seriously by aspiring screenwriters."
—Tony Bill, Coproducer of *The Sting*
Director of *My Bodyguard*
"The complete primer, a step-by-step guide from the first glimmer of an idea to marketing the finished script."
—*New West*

Now brings you—

The Screenwriter's Workbook

*An outstanding, essential guide
to creating screenplays for every
screenwriter serious about his craft*

Books by Syd Field:

The Screenwriter's Workbook

Screenplay: The Foundations of Screenwriting

Selling a Screenplay: The Screenwriter's Guide to Hollywood

Four Screenplays

The Screenwriter's Problem Solver:

How to recognize, identify, and define screenwriting

problems

The Screenwriter's Workbook

Syd Field

A Dell Trade Paperback

Published by
Dell Publishing
a division of
Bantam Doubleday Dell Publishing Group, Inc.
1540 Broadway
New York, New York 10036

Library of Congress Cataloging in Publication Data

Field, Syd.
    The screenwriter's workbook.

    Includes index.
    1. Moving-picture authorship.   I. Title.
PN1996.F44   1984   808.2'03   84-1747
ISBN 0-440-58225-3

Printed in the United States of America

July 1984

30 29 28 27 26 25 24 23 22

BVG

A special thanks to Jean Renoir
for pointing out the path through the forest.

For my students . . .
who taught me everything
I needed to know

*The hardest thing about writing
is knowing what to write.*

Contents

Introduction

Since the publication of *Screenplay* I have traveled exten-
sively throughout the United States, Canada, and Europe
giving screenwriting workshops and seminars to members
of the film industry, professional screenwriters, students,
and people from all walks of life.

They all have one thing in common; they want to write
screenplays.

The first thing they have to do, I tell them, is to give up
the idea that I'm going to teach them *how to* write a screenplay. I can't *teach* anybody how to do anything; if they want
to write a screenplay, I say, then they're going to have to
teach themselves how to do it.

The Screenwriter's Workbook is not a *how-to* book; it is
a *what-to* book. If you have an idea for a screenplay, and
you don't know what to do with it, this book tells you
what you have to do in order to write a successful screenplay.

"How" you do it is up to you.

The Workbook is based on the screenwriting workshops
I conduct in Los Angeles. I design and structure the eight-
week workshops so students spend the first four weeks

preparing to write their material, the second four weeks *writing* it. The goal of the class (and I'm very big on goals) is to write and complete the first 30 pages, or Act I, of the screenplay.

People come into the first class with a short, three-sentence idea of their story. For example: "My story is about a woman executive on vacation in Hawaii, who meets and has an affair with a young man, and returns with him to Los Angeles only to learn the relationship doesn't work."

That simple.

In this first class we talk about dramatic structure and explain the *paradigm*; the students' first assignment is to structure their story line into a four-page treatment focusing on the ending, the beginning, and the first two plot points. I call this a "kick in the ass" exercise because it is probably the most difficult thing the student will write. The second week we talk about character, and the assignment is to write character biographies of two or three main characters. The third week we structure the first act on 3 × 5 cards, and write up the back story, what happens a day, a week, or an hour before the story begins. The fourth week we write the first 10 pages, and the rest of the workshop is devoted to writing 10 pages a week. At the end of this eight-week session, they have completed the first 30 pages, or Act I, of their screenplay.

We take a short break, then continue into the Second Act Workshop; the goal of this eight-week class is to write and complete the second act. In the third workshop they complete Act III and the rewrite.

Almost 80 percent of all my students complete their screenplays. Many of them have extraordinary success. A former student of mine won the Humanitas Award for

Divorce Wars, with Tom Selleck and Jane Curtin; another won the Writer's Guild Best Teleplay Award for her story *The Violation of Sarah MacDavid*; still another wrote *The Thorn Birds* and *The Last Days of Pompeii*. Many students have had their screenplays and teleplays optioned by producers. A few have even become production executives at film studios and production companies.

This book is designed and structured exactly like the screenwriting workshops. The material works. Read a chapter, then do the exercise at the end of the chapter, and by the end of the book you will have written a screenplay. *The Workbook* creates a work plan for you to follow from inception through completion; it is a map, a guide through the screenwriting process.

The exercises that follow each chapter give you an opportunity to expand your screenwriting skills. I hope you will view your progress through the screenwriting experience in this light. You won't learn anything unless you give yourself permission to make some mistakes, to try things that don't work, and do some plain old terrible writing.

Are you willing to do that?

Are you willing to try something that doesn't work? Are you willing to write terrible pages? Are you willing to be lost in doubt and confusion, angry and concerned, not knowing whether your material is working or not?

This book *is* a learning experience.

It is experiential. The more you do, the better you get, like swimming or riding a bicycle.

Read the book, and when you're ready to start working on your screenplay, go through the book a chapter at a time. It is a step-by-step process; you may spend a week, or a month, on a single chapter. Take as much time as you need to complete the material in each exercise.

The purpose of *The Screenwriter's Workbook* is to clarify, expand, and enlarge your knowledge, comprehension, and technique of the screenplay and the art and craft of screenwriting.

The Workbook will give you the opportunity of teaching yourself the necessary skills and craft required to write a screenplay.

That's why it's a *what-to* book. No one's going to teach you *how* to write anything; you're going to teach yourself to do that.

That's what it's all about anyway.

"A man's reach," Robert Browning wrote, "should exceed his grasp."

part one: PREPARATION

1

Where the Writer Begins

Wherein we answer the question of where to begin:

Where *does* the writer begin?

When you sit down and tell yourself you're going to write a screenplay, where do you begin? With a shot of a car streaking down the desert highway? At the racetrack, the crowd in a frenzy? Do you begin in silence, with a clock ticking loudly?

Where *does* the writer begin? It's a question I hear all the time. At workshops and seminars both here and abroad, people tell me they've got a great idea for a screenplay, but they don't know where to begin. Should they write a treatment, outline it, or make notes about it? Do they begin with a person, newspaper article, or title?

Writing a screenplay is a *process,* an organic, ever-changing, continuing stage of development; it is a craft that occasionally rises to the level of art. There are definite stages the writer works through in fleshing out and drama-tizing an idea; the creative process is the same in all writing; only the form is different.

When you sit down to write a screenplay, you're beginning a process that will end months, perhaps years later with some 120 pages filled with words, dialogue, and description in what is called a screenplay.

If you know where the writer begins, you can create a step-by-step approach that will guide you through the entire process of writing a screenplay. That is the purpose of this book.

So—where *does* the writer begin?

With a blank sheet of paper? Yes. But you've got to fill 120 blank sheets of paper with a screenplay. And a screenplay is defined as a story told with pictures in dialogue and description and placed within the context of dramatic structure.

What about starting with character? Yes. Definitely. A strong and appealing character is essential in every screenplay. A full-bodied, three-dimensional character will move your story forward with skill and clarity; it is a good, solid start point, but it's not where the writer begins.

What about starting with an incident or experience that happened to you, or someone you know? Sometimes you can use a particular experience as a start point in your story, but many times you'll find yourself holding on to the "reality" of the experience because you want to be "true" to the situation or incident. And you've got to let the "reality" go so you can dramatize it effectively. "Who did what" and "where it happened" usually end up as a thin story with little or no dramatic value.

With an idea? Definitely, yes, but an idea is only an idea: you've got to dramatize that idea, expand it, clothe it, make it say what you want to say. "I want to write a story about a horse trainer at the Kentucky Derby" is not enough. You don't have enough information with just the idea. You've got to dramatize it.

What about using a place or a location, and starting there? You can do that. Start with a particular place, a location, but it's still not enough: you've got to create a character and situation to build your story.

With plot? A plot about what? Plot is what happens, and since you're sitting down in front of a blank sheet of paper, it should be the furthest thing from your mind. Forget plot at this point. We'll deal with it when it's time to deal with it. First things first.

What about research? What are you going to research? You've got to have a subject to research.

And that's the start point. The subject.

Where does the writer begin?

With a *subject,* and *structure.*

Before you can even prepare to write your screenplay, you must have a definite subject, an *action* and a *character.*

The subject can be as simple as a visitor from outer space missing his spaceship home and being found and befriended by some children, who help him escape. That's *E.T.—The Extra-Terrestrial.* Or the subject can be the heavyweight champion of the world losing his boxing crown and then regaining it (*Rocky III*). Or the subject can be an archeologist recovering a famous document or artifact that has been lost for centuries (*Raiders of the Lost Ark*).

In my screenwriting workshops the first thing I ask people to do is tell me what their story is about. I hear answers like "I'm writing a story about good and evil." That's one of my favorites. Or "I'm writing about three generations of an Irish family in Chicago at the time of the 1968 Democratic convention." Or "I'm writing about a group of people building their own school when their neighborhood school is closed.'' None of these prospective screenplay writers had any idea of what they were going to write. I badgered them to be more specific, and after a couple of weeks they began to focus on a main character and an action. Before you can begin a screenplay, you've got to know your subject—that is, what the screenplay is about—in terms of a character performing a certain line of dramatic or comedic action.

Writing a screenplay is a step-by-step process. One step at a time. First, find the subject, then structure the idea, then do character biographies, then do any research you need, then structure the first act on 3 × 5 cards; then write the screenplay, day by day, first Act I, then Act II and Act III. When the first words-on-paper draft is complete, do basic revisions and changes to reduce it to length, then polish it until it's ready to be shown around. You must be clear every step of the way, and know where you're going and what you're doing. It's very easy to get lost in the words and action of the evolving screenplay.

What *is* your story about? Define it. Articulate it.

Are you writing a love story with a strong action-adventure interest, or are you writing an action-adventure story with a strong love interest? If you don't know, who does?

Who is your main character and what is the action of your story? What happens?

Breaker Morant, based on the play by Kenneth Ross and adapted by Australian writer-director Bruce Beresford, is the story of an Australian military lieutenant in the Boer War (1900) who is court-martialed and executed for fighting the enemy in an ''unorthodox and uncivilized'' fashion (guerrilla warfare). He is convicted and executed for political reasons, a pawn on the chessboard of international politics. His fighting tactics, under orders (denied, of course, by his superiors) had nothing to do with what he did or how he did it.

That is the subject of *Breaker Morant*. The fact that the English army had to make clear to the world they did not permit this sort of unorthodox or "uncivilized" fighting had to be dramatized; they had to have a political scapegoat, so they chose three Australian soldiers. There has to be a fall guy. Just look at the recent Falkland Islands episode, where the prestige of the governments involved was more important than the islands themselves.

Paths of Glory, Stanley Kubrick's exceptional antiwar film, is basically the same subject as *Breaker Morant*. It is the story of three men who are court-martialed and executed for leaving their posts under enemy fire during the First World War.

What is the subject of your screenplay? Reduce your idea into a character and an action in a few sentences, no more than three or four. Remember, this has nothing to do with your screenplay or the accuracy of your story; it is simply a guide for you to follow during the process of writing it.

You have to know what you're writing about. A good example is what happened to a student of mine. A published novelist and editor for a major book publisher, she had never written a screenplay and was nervous and insecure.

Her original idea was to write a story about an active yet elderly woman who suffers a traumatic injury, is hospitalized, does not respond to treatment, falls into a deep depression, and is given electric shock treatments by an overzealous doctor. Fine. My student had a lot of considerations about the story: Was it visual enough? Could she keep the main character in a hospital bed during most of the second act? Was the main character too passive? Could interest be sustained with this limited sense of visual action? All valid, all major considerations, requiring creative decisions.

We discussed it, talked about opening it up, using the visual components found in the hospital: tests like EEGs and X rays, (remember *The Exorcist* brain scan sequence?) the arrival of emergency cases, the activities of nurses on the floor. Feeling secure, my student began preparing her material. She did research, structured the first act, designed the opening. As a novelist, she was used to working by researching the idea and then finding her story and characters through the writing. She lets the story lead her to where it wants to go. Many novelists work this way.

Not screenwriters. A screenplay follows a certain, lean, tight, narrative line of action, a line of development. A screenplay always moves forward, with direction, toward the resolution. You've got to be on track every step of the way; every scene, every fragment, must be taking you somewhere, moving you forward in terms of story development. It's very easy to get lost in the maze of the day-by-day process of writing.

Writing a screenplay is like climbing a mountain. When you're climbing, all you can see is the rock in front of you and the rock directly above you. You can't see where you've come from or where you're going. The same principle holds true when you're writing a screenplay. All you can see is the page you're writing and the pages you've written. You can't see anything beyond that.

After preparing her material, my student started writing. The main character, an elderly woman, was active, likable, and well drawn. But when she entered the hospital at the end of Act I, the *tone* of the story changed. She was now confined to a hospital bed, unconscious for several pages. My student started to write scenes with doctors and nurses, and then brought in the main character's daughter, a woman executive who has trouble dealing with authoritarian male figures like doctors. In Act II the daughter began to emerge as the dominant character. In order to make that work, my student had to shift the basic story line: the story was now about a daughter taking charge of the health and well-being of her mother.

The first words-on-paper—that is, the first draft in screenplay form—seemed to be working well. The story was moving and dramatic. It now hinged upon the idea of "informed consent," an interesting premise in medical therapy: the daughter was asked to choose between electric shock treatments and drug therapy as a means of bringing her mother out of acute depression. Both treatments have disastrous side effects, and the daughter's decision at the end of Act II was to *do nothing,* to wait and see; no shock, no drugs, nothing, just see if her mother would respond in time, with patience and understanding.

The only problem with the first words-on-paper draft was that there were two separate stories. Whose story was it? Was it the story of the mother or the daughter? My student didn't know. So she gave the draft to a close friend of hers, a literary agent in Hollywood. Her friend thought the script needed some work, but liked it enough to give it to one of her associates at the office. He read it and felt that the script was "slow, dull and boring." It should have more action: "Let's *see* her getting an electric shock treatment; change the opening, make it more active."

My student came to me in rage and confusion. She didn't know *what* to do. She kept talking about a more active, cinematic opening. I told her that wasn't the problem;

she had to know what story she was writing—the story of the mother's recovery from the traumatic injury or the story of the daughter's fear of male authority and the need to give "informed consent."

She kept asking me what to do, and I kept telling her she had to make a creative decision about which story she was writing. Before she could begin to rewrite anything she had to rethink her idea from the beginning in order to find the focus and direction of her story.

I suggested she fashion her story into the relationship between the mother and daughter set against the dramatic line of the mother's injury and the need for "informed consent," and to show how this brings them together with love and understanding.

It was not the story she wanted to write. Fine. But she still had to decide whose story it is. She didn't. Lost in doubt and confusion, she finally shelved the project.

It could happen to anyone.

What is the *subject* of your screenplay? What is your story about, in terms of action and character? Write it in a few sentences. Like:

My story is about a careless attorney who meets and falls in love with a married woman, then kills her husband so they can be together. But he's been set up for murder and ends up in prison, while she ends up with a fortune in a tropical paradise. That's the subject of *Body Heat*.

Or: My story is about an American businessman (the main character) who goes to a Latin American country to find out what happened to his son during a military coup and learns he's been killed (the action). That's the subject of *Missing*.

Or: My story is about a professional thief, a loner, who agrees to pull a job for a crime syndicate, only to be double-crossed, then ends up killing everybody and taking back what's his. That's the subject of *Thief*.

What are you writing about? Write it out; it may take you several pages at first. Reduce it to a few sentences focusing on the *subject,* the *action,* and the *character.* It may take several days of thinking before you can even isolate the main components of your story. Don't worry about how long it takes. Just do it.

The subject is the guideline for you to follow as you structure the action and character into a dramatic story line.

Where does the writer begin?

With the subject and structure.

And that brings us to structure.

The Exercise

Take your idea and write it out in three sentences according to action and character. Isolating your main character should present no problems, but defining the line of action may be more difficult. It may help to free-associate about your story line in terms of action. Do not be *specific;* avoid *detail.* Be as *general* as possible.

It may take you three or four pages of writing to define the action and figure out what story you're telling. Now reduce the idea to a few paragraphs. Then reduce this to a few sentences. Say it out loud. Read it out loud. Polish it some more. Do it until you are perfectly clear about your subject and can express it clearly and concisely in three or four sentences.

This is the first step in the screenwriting process.

2

On Structure

Wherein we explore the relationship between structure and the screenplay:

Structure is the most important element in the screenplay. It is the force that holds everything together; it is the skeleton, the spine, the foundation. Without structure, you have no story; without story, you have no screenplay.

Good structure in a screenplay is like an ice cube and water. An ice cube has a definite crystalline structure, separate and different from water. But when an ice cube melts, it becomes indistinguishable from whence it came. It is the same, but different. It should be so integral to your story, so closely connected, you can't see it. All good films have a strong and solid structural foundation.

What *is* structure? I ask that question in my screenwriting workshops and seminars, because I think a thorough knowledge and understanding of structure is essential to writing a screenplay. Yet I find many writers, American and European, professional and amateur, have no intellectual understanding of structure. But they do understand it intuitively. They refer to it in vague generalities and hazy abstractions, talk about the "mystery of structure," and try to describe it like the sun on an overcast day.

A screenplay without structure has no story line; it wanders around, searching for itself, is dull and boring. It doesn't work. It has no direction, no line of development; *9/30/55, American Hot Wax, Honky Tonk Freeway, A Wedding,* and *Health,* are good examples. There is no clear-cut line of dramatic action, only a situation; two parallel lines that never meet.

A good screenplay always has a strong line of dramatic action; it goes somewhere, moves forward, step by step, toward the resolution. If you want to take a trip, you don't get on an airplane or train and then figure out where you're going, do you? You have to go somewhere. You have a destination. You start *here* and end *there*.

That's what structure is all about. It is a tool that lets you shape and form your screenplay with maximum dramatic value. Structure *holds* everything together; all the action, characters, plot, incidents, episodes, and events that make up your screenplay.

As Richard Feynman, the Nobel prize–winning physicist from Cal Tech, has pointed out, the laws of nature are so simple it's hard to see them. In order to do so, we have to rise above our level of complexity and understanding. For example, human beings had been observing natural phenomena for centuries before Newton realized that "for every action there is an equal and opposite reaction." What could be simpler than that?

Structure is like that; it's so simple it's like an ice cube and water, or a fire and its heat.

If you were asked to define structure what would you say? How would you describe it? What does it do? What *is* structure?

One definition of *structure* is "something built or constructed, like a building or dam; the arrangement or interrelation of all the parts of a whole; anything put together systematically; the arrangement of parts or elements.'' It can also be defined as a ''complex system considered from the point of view of the whole rather than any single part; anything composed of parts arranged in some way; an organization; the relationship or organization of the component parts of a work of art or literature.''

The root *struct* means ''to put together.'' Simply put, structure is the relationship between the parts and the whole.

The parts and the whole. This can be illustrated with the game of chess. If you want to play chess you need four elements: a chessboard, a set of chessmen, a pair of players, and agreement on a certain set of rules. If there are no rules, there is no game. The parts and the whole. That's what structure is, the relationship between the parts and the whole.

When you assemble a sound system, you put together certain components: an amplifier, pre-amp, tuner, turntable, speakers, cartridge, cassette deck, and so on. And when you connect them together, you have built a sound system. How good or how bad it is (the whole) depends on the quality of the components (the parts).

At one time, it was said that the whole is nothing more than the sum of its parts. No more. Modern physics challenges that assumption with the general systems theory, a theory that states the whole is *greater* than the sum of its parts.

We see this in sporting events all the time. In the 1981 World Series the Los Angeles Dodgers lost the first two games, then came back to win four games in a row. The Dodgers transcended their individual skills and created a team effort that was greater than the sum of their individual abilities.

In the National Football League, it is said that a team "plays up to the level of its competition." Team play varies from week to week, but when you add the emotional element anything can happen; teams rise above the level of their abilities.

Great beauty is more than just external features; the whole *is* greater than the sum of its parts. The ancient Indian story about the blind men and the elephant illustrates this well. Three blind men are asked to describe an elephant. One man feels the trunk and says an elephant is round, narrow, and flexible, like a snake. The second blind man feels the midsection and says an elephant is like a wall. The third feels the tail and says an elephant is like a piece of rope.

Who is right? The elephant is greater than the sum of its parts. That's the general systems theory.

What does this have to do with screenwriting? Everything. "A screenplay *is* structure," says William Goldman. "It is the spine you hang your story on." When you sit down to write a screenplay, you must approach your story as a whole. A story is composed of parts—characters, plot, action, dialogue, scenes, sequences, incidents, events—and you, as writer, must fashion these "parts" into a "whole," a definite shape and form, complete with beginning, middle, and end.

Structure is the relationship between the parts and the whole. Then what is the relationship between structure and the screenplay? And what *is* a screenplay?

A screenplay is a story told in pictures, dialogue, and description, within the context of dramatic structure.

*   *   *

A screenplay is a story told in pictures: A screenplay deals with visual images, with external *details,* with a man crossing a crowded street, a car turning the corner, an elevator door opening, a woman pushing her way through a crowd. In a screenplay you tell your story with pictures.

A novel is different. A novel usually deals with the inner, interior life of someone, and the character's thoughts, feelings, emotions, and memories take place within the *mindscape* of dramatic action. A novel usually takes place inside a character's head. Open any novel at random and read a chapter or two and you'll see what I mean.

A play is different. A play is told through dialogue, in words, on the stage; the action is performed in the *language* of dramatic action. Characters talk about themselves or other characters or about memories or events in their lives. A play is told in words. Talking heads.

Jean-Luc Godard says that film is evolving into a visual language and we must learn to read the pictures.

I had an experience that illustrates this principle. Taking a break from the European screenwriting workshop in Brussels, I went to Venice and visited the Academia Museum; it displays a magnificent collection of early Venetian painting. In the Middle Ages, when monks in monasteries were transcribing the Scriptures, they enlarged and elaborated the initial letter of a paragraph. (A similar procedure is followed today when the first letter of a chapter is set in large type.) It wasn't long before the monks were illustrating their manuscripts with scenes from the Bible, and soon they were decorating their walls with illustrations similar to Roman frescoes; then these "scenes/paintings" were put on wood panels which leaned against the wall, and this gave way to painting on canvas which then hung on the wall. The Academia Museum displays a marvelous collection of this early Italian painting, which in the beginning was always concerned with religious themes.

As I wandered around the museum, I was struck by one painting in particular; it was composed of 12 individual wood panels depicting scenes in the life of Christ: one panel showed his birth, another the Sermon on the Mount, another the Last Supper, and then the Crucifixion, and so on. Something about this painting grabbed me, held my interest, and I didn't know why. I stared at that painting for a long time, thinking about it, then moved away, and found myself coming back to it, interested, intrigued. What made this painting different from all the others? The answer came immediately: it wasn't just *one* painting. It was a series of 12 paintings mounted together to tell the story of the life and death of Christ. It was a story told in pictures.

It blew me away. The interaction between story and picture in each panel was the same as the visual relationship between story and character in a screenplay, the same relationship between an ice cube and water.

I stared at the panel for a long time, suddenly seeing the connection between painting and film. It was a stunning and dramatic moment. Everything exists in relationship to something else, and I remembered something Jean Renoir, the great French film director, told me. He said that "learning" is "being able to see the relationship between things."

I suddenly understood what he meant.

. . . *in dialogue and description:* A screenplay is a story told in word and picture; characters communicate certain facts and information to the reader; dialogue comments on the action, sometimes *is* the action, and always moves the story forward.

When you write a scene or sequence, you are describing what your character says and does—the incidents and events that tell your story. When you write a screenplay, you are describing what happens, which is why screenplays are written in the present tense. The reader sees what the CAMERA sees, a description of the action placed . . .

. . . *within the context of dramatic structure:* Your screenplay has a definite structure, a beginning, middle, and end, even if it's told in flashback, like *Annie Hall.* Your story starts *here* and ends *there;* it goes from point A to point Z.

Structure *is* a context because it "holds" everything together. *Context,* remember, is illustrated by an empty coffee cup. If you take an empty cup, look inside it, you will see a space. That space *holds* the *content*—coffee, tea, milk, water, beer, lemonade, orange drink, apple juice, or whatever—in place. *Context* always holds *content* in place, the same way that structure *holds* your story in place.

And *dramatic structure* is defined as "a linear arrangement of related incidents, episodes, and events leading to a dramatic resolution."

Why is structure so important? Because it is a *tool* that helps you build your story into a dramatic form. It is a start point in the process of writing.

The Exercise

This is a workbook. It provides you with the opportunity to improve your screenwriting abilities. To do that, it is important for you to evaluate your skills and weaknesses as a screenwriter. This exercise is a self-inventory.

Take a sheet of paper and, in a few paragraphs, evaluate and define your skills as a screenwriter. In your screenwriting or other writing experience, what would you say your strong points are? Your weak points? (If you've never written anything before, why do you think you can write a screenplay?) Be honest with yourself. What would you like to improve? Would you like to write better dialogue? Create deeper, more three-dimensional characters? Do you want a better grasp and understanding of structure? Of plot?

What would you like to improve upon? Just write it out. Put down your thoughts and feelings about your abilities as a screenwriter. Don't worry about grammar, spelling, or punctuation. No one is going to see this but you, so be as truthful as you can about what skills you want to improve upon. Do it, then put it away and forget about it.

The Workbook is experiential; the more you put in, the more you get out.

3

The Paradigm

Wherein we redefine the paradigm:

The *paradigm* is dramatic structure. It is a tool, a guide, a map through the screenwriting process. As defined in *Screenplay,* a *paradigm* is a "model, an example, a conceptual scheme."

The more I learn about the *paradigm* and its function in the screenwriting process, the more amazed I am at how important it really is. In science, systems are referred to as open or closed. A closed system is like a rock—it takes nothing from its environment and gives nothing back. There is no interchange between the rock and its surroundings.

An open system is like a city: it interacts with its environment, and there is an exchange between them. The city depends on the surrounding areas for food and raw materials, and people in those areas depend on the city for trade and other services. There is a give-and-take exchange between the city and its surroundings.

A screenplay is an open system. You plan what you're going to write—"Bill leaves Grace's apartment and takes a long walk through the city"—but it may not work out that way. Bill may "tell you" he doesn't want to go on a long walk through the city—he wants music, dancing, drugs, women. When that happens, *you* better listen.

Writing a screenplay is an adventure, and you're never quite sure how it's going to turn out. It is an open system.

Teaching is an open system. The teacher presents material to the students; they listen, question, doubt, argue, and finally assimilate it, *causing* the original material to expand and evolve into *new* material. That's what happened to the *paradigm* after *Screenplay* was first published. (See Chapter 11, "The New Paradigm.")

The more I illustrate and describe the *paradigm* in screenwriting workshops, the more I learn how valuable and effective and important it really is in the screenwriting process. The *paradigm* is a model, an example, a conceptual scheme.

The *paradigm* of a table, for example, is "a top with four legs." Within that paradigm you can have a short table, long table, high table, low table. You can have a square table, round table, octagonal table, rectangular table, glass table, chrome table, wrought-iron table, wood table, plastic table, and so on, and the *paradigm* of a table still holds true: "a top with four legs."

It is a *model*. If you are building a new house, or remodeling an old one, you hire an architect or designer to draw up blueprints, preliminary plans, and working plans. And unless you have been trained to read such plans, you have trouble visualizing what the house is going to look like. Lines on paper are not really walls and ceilings. We need to *see* the work before we can make any kind of aesthetic decision.

A model is built to scale. It doesn't matter whether it's a house, building, swimming pool, tennis court, car, bus, or boat, we need to *see* it. We need a model.

When scientists explore the mysteries of the atom, they build models to show what it looks like: a nucleus with protons and neutrons, surrounded by rings of electrons. When scientists at the Jet Propulsion Laboratory receive data from the *Voyager* spacecraft monitoring different worlds, they take the measurement results and construct models of Mars, Io, and Jupiter to see what they look like. Then they can theorize about what natural laws are at work.

The *paradigm* is a model, an example, a conceptual scheme of what a screenplay looks like. It is a *whole,* comprising *parts*:

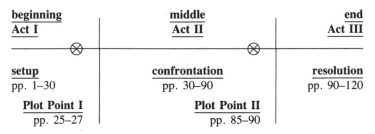

beginning	middle	end
Act I	**Act II**	**Act III**
setup	**confrontation**	**resolution**
pp. 1–30	pp. 30–90	pp. 90–120
Plot Point I	**Plot Point II**	
pp. 25–27	pp. 85–90	

We know a screenplay is "a story told with pictures, in dialogue and description, and placed within the context of dramatic structure," but what is a story? And what do all stories have in common?

A beginning, middle, and end. The beginning corresponds to Act I, the middle to Act II, and the end to Act III.

The average movie is about two hours long, or 120 minutes. Some are longer, some shorter, but they are close to two hours. One written page of screenplay equals one minute of screen time.

(You may want to check this out. Read a screenplay, then see the movie and determine if it's true or not! If you're seriously interested in writing a screenplay, you should be reading all the scripts you can get your hands on, and seeing all the movies you can afford. In a movie theater if possible.)

Act I, the beginning, is a unit, or block, of dramatic (or comedic) action, that is 30 pages long. It begins on page one and continues on to the plot point at the end of Act I. It is held together by the dramatic context known as the *setup*. Act II is a unit, or block, of dramatic (or comedic) action, that goes from page 30 to page 90, from the plot point at the end of Act I to the plot point at the end of Act II. It is 60 pages long, and held together with the dramatic context known as *confrontation*. Act III is also a unit of dramatic or comedic action; it goes from page 90 to page 120, or from the plot point at the end of Act II to the end of your script. It is a unit that is 30 pages long, and held together with the dramatic context known as *resolution*.

There are some variations, of course. In *Chinatown* and *Annie Hall,* Act I is 23 or 24 pages long, and sometimes the second act is longer than 60 pages, and there are times when Act III is 20 or 25 pages long.

So what? The *paradigm* still works. Each act is a unit, or block, of dramatic action.

Act I is a unit of dramatic action that *sets up* your story. In the first 30 pages of screenplay, you must set up your story: introduce your main characters, establish your dramatic premise, create the situation, and lay out scenes and sequences that build and expand the information of your story.

Everything in Act I *sets up* your story. You don't have time for cheap tricks and cute and clever scenes and dialogue; you've got to set up your story immediately, from page one. That's why the dramatic context of Act I is the setup. (*Context,* remember, holds the *content* in place, all the scenes, dialogue, description, shots, and special effects that make up a screenplay.) Everything in this unit of action sets up everything to follow.

A perfect example is *An Unmarried Woman,* written and directed by Paul Mazursky. Act I establishes the *marriage* of Jill Clayburgh: we see her jogging with her husband, Michael Murphy, sending her daughter off to school, enjoying a "quickie" with her husband, working part time in an art gallery, having lunch with her best friends, most of whom are divorced and bitter about men. They envy Jill Clayburgh's marriage. Mazursky sets up the character of Jill Clayburgh in the first act, doing it with visual bits and pieces of information about who she is and what she wants.

Jill Clayburgh's marriage sets up her story as an unmarried woman. Like this:

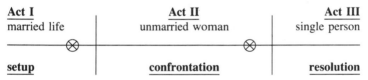

Act I	Act II	Act III
married life	unmarried woman	single person
setup	confrontation	resolution

The same with *Body Heat,* written and directed by Larry Kasdan, one of the finest writer-directors in Hollywood. (He cowrote *The Empire Strikes Back, Return of the Jedi, The Big Chill,* and wrote *Raiders of the Lost Ark.*) The first act deals with setting up Ned Racine (William Hurt). The first words of the script, "Flames in a night sky," set the tone of passion for character and story, and indeed, we first see Ned Racine after his one-night stand with a local Avis rent-a-car girl. Then we see him in court as a practicing attorney, likable but unprepared and shoddy in presentation, a hustler on the lookout for an easy score.

When he first sees Matty Walker (Kathleen Turner) at a concert, he's attracted to her immediately (he's "run by his dick," his best friend says later), and soon is driven by passion and lust in his pursuit until he can't see anything anymore. This paves the way for him to kill her husband in the hopes of scoring a "great piece of ass" and a substantial amount of money. It's the "easy score" he's been searching for, and it's all set up in Act I.

About page 25, a plot point occurs; a *plot point* is an incident, episode, or event that "hooks" into the action and spins it around into another direction, "direction" being a "line of development."

A plot point can be anything: a shot, a speech, a scene, a sequence, an action, anything that moves the story forward. (See Chapter 9 in *Screenplay*.)

In *An Unmarried Woman* everything *seems* fine in Jill Clayburgh's marriage: she is the envy of her friends. On page 25 of the script she is having lunch with her husband, planning their summer vacation. He is distant, wrapped in his own thoughts. They leave the restaurant, but as they are walking down the street, the husband suddenly breaks down and bursts into tears.

"What is it?" Jill Clayburgh asks. "What's wrong?"

I've met another woman, I've fallen in love, and I want a divorce, he says.

That's a plot point—an incident, episode, or event that "hooks" into the action and spins it around into another direction.

On page 9 of *Body Heat* Ned Racine meets Matty Walker; during their conversation she tells him, "I'm a married woman."

"Meaning what?" he responds.

"Meaning I'm not looking for company."

"Then you should have said 'I'm a *happily* married woman.' " He knows at that moment she is available to him—what she says and what she means are two different things. Later, when she invites him back to her house to "hear the wind chimes," he promises "nothing will happen." He tries to keep his word, but his flesh is frail, and when he leaves the house and stands at his car debating whether to drive off or not, he looks at the lovely woman through the glass front door and, blinded by lust, breaks through the window and takes her right there, on the floor at the foot of the stairs.

Plot Point I occurs when they come together, establishing a relationship that will soon lead to murder. It takes us into Act II.

Act II is a unit, or block, of dramatic or comedic action that is 60 pages long and held together by the dramatic context known as *confrontation*. It goes from Plot Point I to Plot Point II. During this section of your script, your main character will confront obstacles and conflicts that must be resolved and overcome in order for your character to achieve his or her dramatic need.

Drama is conflict; without conflict there is no action, without action, no character, without character, no story, without story, no screenplay.

Act II is the unit of action in which your character confronts and overcomes (or does not overcome) all obstacles to achieve his or her dramatic need. If you know what your main character wants to win, gain, get, or achieve during the course of your screenplay (the dramatic need), your story becomes your character overcoming all obstacles to achieve his or her dramatic need.

Everything you do, every scene you write, every shot

you describe, every sequence you devise, is held together by the dramatic context of *confrontation*.

Act II is the most difficult act to write because it is the longest unit of dramatic action. (With the new material presented in this workbook, Act II is broken down into workable units of action. More about this in Chapter 11, "The New Paradigm.")

Act II of *An Unmarried Woman* deals with Jill Clayburgh as an unmarried woman after seventeen years of marriage. She feels betrayed, abandoned, angry, and bitter at men. It is an enormous change, and she finds it difficult adjusting. She must learn how to deal with her new life. She enters therapy, learns how to be a single parent, and soon overcomes her anger at men (focusing it on her husband, where it belongs). She begins to experiment sexually.

At the end of Act II she meets Alan Bates at an art gallery and goes to bed with him, but when he asks to see her again, she refuses, saying she's still experimenting and doesn't want to enter into anything serious. "Nothing personal," she adds.

A few nights later she meets Alan Bates again at a party. They talk, enjoy each other's company, and decide to leave the party together. Despite what she said at the end of their sexual encounter, she likes him and he likes her, and soon they are in a relationship. The plot point at the end of Act II is their decision to leave the party together; it occurs on page 88. It "spins the action around into another direction." Act III focuses on the new relationship with Alan Bates. This is the way it looks on the *paradigm*:

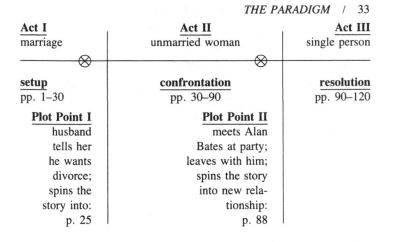

Act I marriage	**Act II** unmarried woman	**Act III** single person
setup pp. 1–30	**confrontation** pp. 30–90	**resolution** pp. 90–120
Plot Point I husband tells her he wants divorce; spins the story into: p. 25	**Plot Point II** meets Alan Bates at party; leaves with him; spins the story into new rela- tionship: p. 88	

The plot point at the end of Act II "spins the story around" into Act III.

In *Body Heat* the plot point at the end of Act II occurs 85 minutes into the film, when Racine's best friend, Lowenstein, tells him someone is trying to implicate him in the murder. "Someone's putting you in deep trouble, my friend. From about 3:30 to 5 A.M. on the night of the murder someone called your hotel room repeatedly. . . . The phone rang and rang but you didn't answer. . . . Now someone's trying to give us Edmund's glasses."

Body Heat is like the mating dance of the black widow spider. When the female black widow is ready to mate, she entices the male to her, by scent and movement, and possibly a web configuration. The male approaches unhesitatingly, they have their mating dance, and they mate. When the female knows her eggs are fertilized, she zaps the male. He's done his job and is not needed anymore.

Such is nature.

We learn, as Ned Racine learns, that Matty has forged her husband's will and is setting up Racine to take the rap.

The plot point "spins" the story around into Act III and we follow Racine's action, step by step, until his betrayal is complete. He ends up behind bars for murder one and on death row, and she ends up in a tropical paradise.

On the paradigm it looks like this:

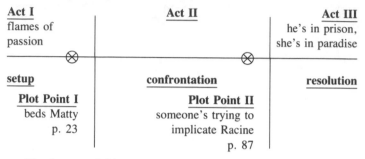

Act I	Act II	Act III
flames of passion		he's in prison, she's in paradise
setup	confrontation	resolution
Plot Point I beds Matty p. 23	Plot Point II someone's trying to implicate Racine p. 87	

She has used him.

The function and purpose of a plot point is simply to *move the story forward*. It is an incident, episode, or event that hooks into the action and spins the story around into another direction.

Do all films have plot points? All films that "work" have a strong, organic structure with plot points clearly defined.

There can be as many as 15 or 20 different plot points in your screenplay: there could be two in Act I, 10 in Act II, and one in Act III. When you first begin to prepare your story for screenplay, however, you must know four things in order to structure your idea: ending, beginning, Plot Point I, and Plot Point II. Once you know these four basic components, you can begin to build and expand your story line.

Act III is a unit of dramatic action that is 30 pages long; it goes from the plot point at the end of Act II to the end. Act III deals with the dramatic context of *resolution*. In

Act III your story resolves itself, resolution being defined as "the solution."

What is the solution to your story? Does your character live or die, succeed or fail, go on a trip or not, get the promotion or not, get married or divorced, or not, survive the test or not, get away safely or not? You must resolve your story. You must know how your story ends. What *is* the resolution to your story? If you don't know, who does?

The *paradigm* is a model, an example, a *whole*:

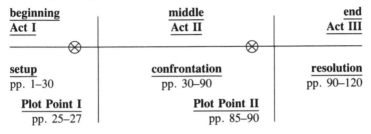

beginning	middle	end
Act I	**Act II**	**Act III**
setup	confrontation	resolution
pp. 1–30	pp. 30–90	pp. 90–120
Plot Point I	**Plot Point II**	
pp. 25–27	pp. 85–90	

It *is* structure, and dramatically it establishes the relationship between the whole and its parts. Dramatic structure is "a linear arrangement of related incidents, episodes, and events, leading to a dramatic resolution."

It is the very foundation of your screenplay.

The Exercise

Before you can express your story dramatically, you must know four things: ending, beginning, Plot Point I, and Plot Point II. These four elements are the structural foundation of your screenplay. You "hang" your entire story around these four elements.

Suppose you have an idea:

> A YOUNG WOMAN in an unhappy marriage, a painter, enrolls in an art class and has an affair with her teacher. Against her will, she falls in love, then learns she is pregnant. Torn between husband and lover, she decides to leave both and raise her child by herself.

The first thing to do with your *subject*—the *action* and *character*—is to structure it: Where do you begin?

With the *paradigm*:

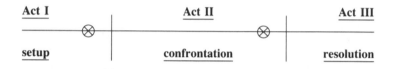

Act I	**Act II**	**Act III**
setup	confrontation	resolution

What's the ending of your story? Where the young woman goes off to have her child by herself, leaving both husband and lover much like Nora in Ibsen's *A Doll House*. That's the end.

What about the beginning? We want the audience to know that the young woman is in an unhappy marriage, so we must *show* this. What kind of scene or sequence would reveal an unhappy marriage? Is the woman's husband an alcoholic? Is he a macho? A weak, emotionless man? What kind of scene could communicate that directly to the audience? In bed? At a party? Preparing for an evening out? Antonioni opened *L'Eclisse* in a living room at dawn. The room is a mess, curtains drawn, ashtrays overflowing, glasses on the table, and a fan in the foreground whirring incessantly. Monica Vitti and her lover (Alain Delon) stare at each other in silence. They have nothing left to say to each other; everything has been said that could have been said. We see immediately their relationship is over.

Determine to open with a scene that will illustrate, or reveal, your dramatic premise.

Think about it. Try out several. See if what you want to work will work. Does it take place during the day or at night? Morning or afternoon? At work or at play?

What about Plot Point I? If Act I sets up the unhappy marriage, the plot point at the end of Act I is where the woman enrolls in the art class. This incident leads to the relationship with her art teacher; it "spins" the story into another direction.

What about Plot Point II? Plot Point I, at the end of Act I, begins the relationship with her teacher that ultimately leads to her becoming pregnant. Plot Point II, at the end of Act II, is the discovery that she is pregnant; this discovery precipitates the action that leads to the resolution, the "solution" to her story: she leaves both husband and lover.

Once you know these four elements ending, beginning, Plot Point I, and Plot Point II, draw the *paradigm*:

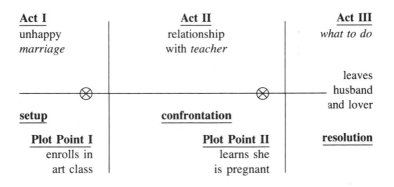

Act I	**Act II**	**Act III**
unhappy	relationship	*what to do*
marriage	with *teacher*	
		leaves
⊗	⊗	husband
		and lover
setup	**confrontation**	
Plot Point I	**Plot Point II**	**resolution**
enrolls in	learns she	
art class	is pregnant	

That's what your idea should "look like" structured. The *paradigm,* remember, is a conceptual tool; it enables you to "see" your story line clearly.

Do the exercise on the following page; structure the story into a dramatic story line.

Start with the ending. Write it on the *paradigm.* Then, how are you going to open it? Where? At the botanist's home? The university? Preparing for the journey? Write it down. Don't worry about its being the "perfect" opening. Just do it.

What about Plot Point I? Is it where he reaches the river, and the trip begins? Is it where the raft overturns? You decide. Structure the idea on the *paradigm.* Play around with it.

Don't get too specific; just lay it out in broad, general strokes. You can fill in the details later.

This exercise is designed to prepare you to structure your own idea so you can move into the next stage in the screenwriting process.

The Paradigm Structured

The story: A well-known BOTANIST sets out with two assistants to explore and catalogue the plants along a certain area of the Colorado River in the Grand Canyon. But their raft is overturned running Upset Rapid and the botanist is severely injured. One of his assistants hikes out to seek help and returns safely.

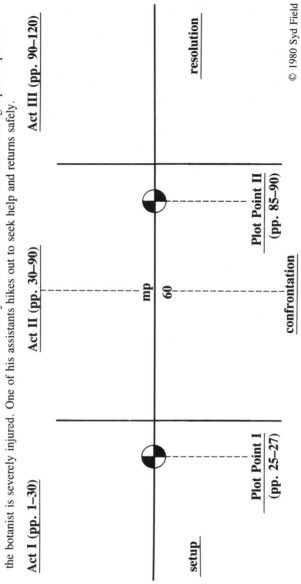

Act I (pp. 1–30)   Act II (pp. 30–90)   Act III (pp. 90–120)

Plot Point I
(pp. 25–27)

mp
60

Plot Point II
(pp. 85–90)

setup

confrontation

resolution

© 1980 Syd Field

4

Four Pages

Wherein we structure the subject into a dramatic story line:

Before you can write anything, you must know four things: the ending, the beginning, Plot Point I, and Plot Point II.

Once you've structured your subject into these four elements you can tell your story in a dramatic, narrative fashion. In fact, narrative means telling a story and implies a sense of direction, a movement, a line of motion from beginning to end.

Putting your story down on paper is essential at this stage; it begins a creative process that is part of the evolution of your screenplay, a necessary stage in fleshing out the development of your idea. How accurate it will be in terms of the finished screenplay, five or six months from now, or how good or bad it is, is irrelevant.

Why is writing a treatment so important? "If you don't know your story, who does?"

Have you heard someone say they have a "great idea" for a screenplay?

"What's it about?" you might ask.

"Well," they begin, "it's about a guy in the Sahara Desert. It opens with a shot of dust rising out of the desert.

Then we see a jeep racing across the sand. Suddenly, the engine sputters, coughs, and slowly dies. Two people in the front seat: a man and a woman. The man climbs out of the jeep, looks around. Isn't that a great idea?''

You nod your head.

"Then what happens?" you ask.

"The rest of the story comes out in the plot. I haven't figured that out yet."

Sure. How many times have you heard that before? What plot?

I've heard that for years from professionals and nonprofessionals alike. They can't tell you any more about the story because they don't *know* any more about it; they haven't defined it yet. Before you can start with your screenplay you've got to define your story.

What's it about? Briefly. What's your subject? Can you state what it's about in a few sentences?

That's why it's necessary to write up a short, four-page treatment. The treatment allows you to see your story with a sense of overview and clarity that you will not have for many months to come.

I emphasize this in my workshops and seminars: "If you don't know your story, who does?" And I illustrate this with an experience out of my own screenwriting career.

I was a freelance screenwriter for seven years, during which time I wrote nine screenplays, mostly originals. (Two were produced. Four were optioned—a producer paid me a certain sum of money so he could have the exclusive right, for one year, to put the movie together, after which time the rights reverted back to me. Nothing happened with the other three.)

The way I worked was simple: I would get an idea and research it; get books from the library and talk to people about it until I felt comfortable with the material. Then I would do my character work, write character biographies, talk to more people, look at pictures. Then I would sit down and start writing. I used to call it "hitting my head against the typewriter." I always came up with a script, but the cost, both physically and emotionally, was very high. It was a slow and painful process, and after years of working this way, I began to look at screenwriting as something I *had* to do rather than something I *wanted* to do. There's a big difference between the two; one is a negative experience, the other positive. While it's important to see both sides, writing is too hard a job, too demanding a task, to add a negative or painful experience to it.

Writing should be an adventure, shrouded in mystery and uncertainty, blessed with amazing grace.

In theory, of course.

The last screenplay I wrote was a painful, but liberating, experience. It also turned out to be beneficial.

I was writing an original script, a western, about a man who rode with Butch Cassidy and the Sundance Kid for several years. But when Butch and Sundance left for South America in 1902, my character stayed behind, refusing to believe the times were changing. He pulled a couple of holdups, was caught, sentenced to prison.

That was the basic idea. I wanted to open the script with my character breaking out of prison after serving four years. After he escapes, he teams up with his old partner, adds a few young members to the gang, and begins to pursue his old way of life. But it is now 1907, and times *have* changed. Banks are using checks, stocks and bonds have become negotiable securities, and you can call from Denver to San Francisco on something called the telephone.

My character can't understand that. He pulls a few jobs, but his expectations are thwarted because nothing works: in one job all he gets is a bundle of checks and a thousand-dollar bill which he can't cash. Another job nets only a hundred dollars in coins and some stock certificates. He doesn't know what to do or where to go, and the Pinkerton detectives are closing in on him. My character plans one last job, a big one, pulls it off, but the money is left behind; he and his partner manage to escape with their lives. In the end, they talk about going to South America to join Butch and Sundance, but they've just been killed.

That's about all I knew when I sat down and began writing, "hitting my head against the typewriter."

This time it didn't work.

Or, I should say, it worked for about 30 pages, and after that I didn't know what happened, or what to do or where to go, and after struggling with the story line for several weeks I plunged into the infamous writer's block.

It was awful. To help me I started doing a lot of drugs, but instead of finding my story I simply got further and further away from it. I became angry, despondent, and frustrated, then surrendered to a deep depression. It went on for several weeks. Until I became frightened, and at that moment stopped taking everything. Cold turkey.

A few days later a friend of mine, then story editor for Lorimar Productions, called, and we went out to dinner. Aware of the "problem," he asked me a very simple question—"What's your story about?"

I looked at him dumbfounded; in all my despair and pain and depression over my "writing block" I had forgotten all about my story. It was the first time I was being asked to tell the story, to describe it out loud.

I stammered awhile trying to remember what it was

about, finally managed to blurt out the basic idea. He listened, asked some pertinent questions, made some suggestions, and told me he wanted to see something in writing, a short treatment.

I agreed, and when I returned that night, I sat down and wrote a short *treatment*—a narrative synopsis of the story told in 4 to 20 pages and using some dialogue.

I couldn't believe what happened; as soon as I knew my story, my writer's block vanished.

That's when I suddenly understood: "The hardest thing about writing is knowing what to write."

In my screenwriting workshops and seminars across the United States, Canada, and Europe, I stress the fact that you must know your story before you can write anything; that means knowing the four basic structural components that "hold" your story together: ending, beginning, Plot Point I, and Plot Point II. When you know these four elements you can write your idea into a dramatic story line in four pages.

Why four pages and not 10 or 20?

Because at this stage you don't know very much about your story; you only have the subject—an action and a character. There's no way you can begin to write a good 10- or 20-page treatment.

You might believe that the more you know about your story now, the better off you'll be later. That's true later, not now. At this point you don't know very much about your story. As you begin writing, you'll add in, or color, a lot of details: In this scene, where is your character coming from? Why is he or she here? What day does your character go into the bank? Why does your character do this and not that?

It's fine to know some of this, but don't get carried

away with excessive detail. Too much detail now is not going to serve your best interests. You'll always be able to add detail later on, such as what kind of a car he drives, why she goes by train and not plane, or why do they go to Mexico and not Europe. You don't need to know that *right now*. Later on, yes.

That's why a four-page treatment is a perfect length at this stage; it gives you the impression of a story, with a sense of direction. After all, it's simply a *start point* in the screenwriting process. So put away your expectations, get them out of sight, and simply sit down and write the story.

The Exercise

Draw the *paradigm*. This is the way it should look: (see facing page).

Then take the subject of your story—the action and character—and lay it all out in dramatic structure; choose your ending first, then your beginning, then Plot Point I and Plot Point II. Do it the same way you did the structure exercise in the previous chapter.

Examine your story line. What's your opening? Where does it take place? In a car, on a deserted road, in the back country, a crowded city street, an empty elevator? Don't be too specific or precise; you don't have to know *everything* yet. Just deal with your story line in broad generalities.

If your opening takes place at the office, what is your character doing? Arriving at work on Monday morning? Leaving on Friday afternoon? Sketch it in, knowing you can change it later. Remember that the purpose of this

The Paradigm Structured

The Story:

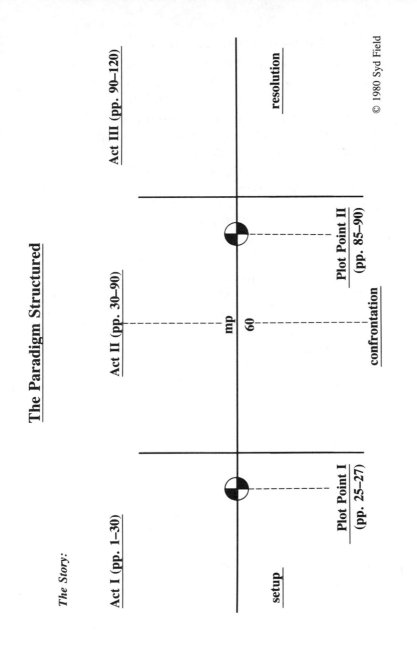

© 1980 Syd Field

Act I (pp. 1–30)

Act II (pp. 30–90)

Act III (pp. 90–120)

Plot Point I (pp. 25–27)

mp
60

Plot Point II (pp. 85–90)

setup

confrontation

resolution

exercise is to dramatize and define your story line in four pages. Double spaced.

Not eight pages, or five pages. Four pages.

Once you've decided on your *opening,* sit down and write the narrative action that opens the story—about *half a page.* For example: "Night. A car slowly weaves through the streets. It turns a corner, the lights go out, and it coasts to a stop in front of a large office building. Silence. In the distance, a dog barks. JOE sits silently behind the wheel, a radio transmitter on the seat next to him. He slips on a pair of earphones, slowly turns the dial to pick up police calls. Then he sits. And waits."

And that's only the first paragraph. We haven't hit the opening yet; we've just set it up.

Continue writing the opening sequence, dramatizing the action in broad, general terms. Remember, writing a narrative synopsis means telling your story; it implies a sense of direction, a movement, or motion, from beginning to end.

Use a few lines of dialogue if you need to.

You are telling a story first, writing a screenplay second.

Write the opening sequence in about *half a page.* In the next half page, the remainder of page one, write a couple of paragraphs describing the action that takes you to the plot point at the end of Act I. Our main character, the botanist, for example, might be taking the river trip. The plot point at the end of Act I will be when the character reaches the river and begins the journey.

When you complete the action leading to Plot Point I, you have the first page of your four-page treatment; it dramatizes the action in Act I.

On page two, write the plot point at the end of Act I, just the way you did when you were writing the opening. Where does it take place? Describe it. If our character arrives at the river, when does he arrive? What does he do—check into a hotel, meet his associates, have dinner, check the provisions? Write it out, focusing on Plot Point I, and describe the action in about *half a page*.

Once again, do not be too specific; do not use much detail; simply describe the action—that is, what happens—in broad strokes.

Now you're ready to move into the second act. Act II is a unit of dramatic action that is 60 pages long. It begins at the plot point at the end of Act I and goes to the plot point at the end of Act II. It is held together with the dramatic context known as *confrontation*. During the action of the second act, your character will be overcoming obstacles to achieve his or her *dramatic need*. If you know your character's need—what he or she wants to win, gain, get, or achieve during the course of your screenplay—you can create obstacles to that need. Your story becomes your character overcoming all obstacles (or not overcoming them) to achieve his or her dramatic need.

Think about Act II for a moment. Where is your story going? What happens to your main character or characters from Plot Point I to Plot Point II? Then choose two or three major obstacles that will generate conflict within the progression of your story. If your story is about the botanist in the Grand Canyon, possible obstacles might be the dangers of running the white water rapids, succumbing to the tremendous heat; it could be physical hardship and strain; it could be the raft overturning, losing supplies, or friction between the other characters. Choose two or three of these incidents, making sure they move your story *forward* to the plot point at the end of Act II.

Write the action of Act II in about a page, focusing on your character confronting these obstacles; be general, and avoid excessive detail.

When you finish, you've written about two and a half pages, and you're ready to write the plot point at the end of Act II. What is your plot point at the end of the second act? Describe it. Dramatize it. Write it in about *half a page*. Use a few lines of dialogue if necessary. How does the plot point at the end of Act II "spin" the action around into Act III? Keep the story flowing smoothly without regard to specifics. Your tendency will be to add detail, so watch out for it and don't get caught up in it. You'll know when you're doing it because you'll be spending time trying to decide exactly how "it" happens; what the motivation is, or what kind of car, job, location, excuse, or mistake to use. Just let it go. You don't need too much motivation for this exercise. Write the plot point at the end of Act II in *half a page*.

That takes you to Act III, the *resolution*. You have about three pages at this point. What happens in Act III? What happens to your main character that resolves your story? What is the solution? How does it end? Not the specifics, only the generalities. Does your character live or die? Succeed or fail? Get married or divorced?

Write it. Describe the resolution simply. You'll be able to do this in less than half a page.

When you finish this, you'll have your story line written up and dramatized in four pages:

one half page describing the opening scene or sequence;
one half page describing the general action of Act I;
one half page that describes the plot point at the end of Act I;
one half page for the action of Act II;
one half page for the plot point at the end of Act II; and
three quarters to one page for Act III, the resolution.

That's a four-page treatment. It may take you two or three times to write it in four pages. Your first effort may be eight pages, which you'll reduce to five, then cut to four.

These four pages might be the toughest pages you'll write during the entire screenplay. I call it "the kick in the ass exercise" because you are taking an unformed and undefined idea and structuring it in terms of beginning, middle, and end. You might experience all kinds of resistance in writing it; you might get angry and bored, and you will probably make a lot of judgments about what you're writing. Judgments like "This is one of the most boring stories in the world!" or "I hate it! It's simple and stupid!" or "I've heard it all before."

You may be right. Your story may be terrible.

So what? This is a four-page treatment. It has nothing to do with your final screenplay. It's an idea, not the finished product. Your story will change and grow during the writing, so don't think these pages have to be perfect. Forget about your expectations. Support yourself now, and do not make too many critical evaluations. (Save them for later!) Writing is experiential; the more you do the easier it gets.

This is a words-on-paper exercise, nothing more. I tell

students in my workshops and seminars to write four terrible pages. It's okay to write these pages and not have them perfect: they don't have to be carved in stone.

Do the best you can. But *do* the exercise. Write your story line in four pages. It is the start point of the screenwriting process.

5

What Makes a Good Character?

Wherein we isolate and define the qualities of creating character:

What makes a good character?

Motivation? Dialogue? Believability? Yes, definitely.

But these are only parts, or aspects of character; not the whole, or *context* of character.

Think about it. What does make a good character?

F. Scott Fitzgerald wrote in one of his journals that "when you begin with an individual, you create a type." His first novel, *This Side of Paradise,* written when he was 22 or 23, portrayed a dazzling heroine modeled after his wife, Zelda. The book quickly became a best seller, and it wasn't long before the "type" created by Fitzgerald was celebrated in the movies, especially in the movies of Clara Bow, who became famous as the "It" girl. Women all over the country imitated her, dressed like her, styled their hair like hers, acted and talked like her. She typified the flapper, truly a phenomenon of the twenties.

The flapper is a type. So was the flower child a type, celebrated by the Beatles and Bob Dylan in the sixties.

These performers influenced an entire generation. Long hair became the fashion, antiwar demonstrations became commonplace, and flower children were everywhere.

Good character is the heart and soul and nervous system of your screenplay. It is through your characters that the viewers experience emotions, through your characters that they are touched.

Creating a good character is essential to the success of your screenplay; without character you have no action; without action, no conflict; without conflict, no story; without story, no screenplay.

We writers are part and parcel of our characters. "When you create the characters," writes Harold Pinter, "they observe you, their writer, warily. It may sound absurd but I've suffered two kinds of pain from my characters. I have witnessed their pain when I'm in the act of distorting or falsifying them, and I've suffered pain when I've been unable to get to the quick of them, when they willfully elude me, when they withdraw into the shadows.

"There's no question a conflict takes place between the writer and his characters. On the whole I would say the characters are the winners, and that is as it should be. When a writer sets out a blueprint for his characters and keeps them rigidly to it, where they do not at any time upset his applecart, when he has mastered them he has also killed or rather terminated their births."

When you create your characters, you must know them inside and out, their hopes and dreams and fears, their likes and dislikes, background and mannerisms.

What's the best way to approach creating character? There are many ways. Let's start at the beginning.

When we talk about creating character, what are we talking about?

Philosophers talk about a man's life as being measured by the sum total of his actions; our lives are "measured" by what we accomplish, or do not accomplish, in our lifetime. "Life consists in action," Aristotle said, "and its end is a mode of action, not a quality."

What *is* character?

Action is character—what a person does is what he is, not what he says.

In *The Hustler*, written by Sidney Carroll and Robert Rossen, from the book by Walter Tevis, Paul Newman plays Fast Eddie Felson, a smooth-talking, fast-shooting pool player from Oakland. Fast Eddie comes to town to take on the "king of straight pool," Minnesota Fats (Jackie Gleason). Though a better player, Fast Eddie is a "loser." During the story, he goes from being a loser to being a winner. That is his action.

Annie Hall is the story of a man who wants to keep and maintain a relationship with a woman; that is his action. But when she leaves him for another man, he can't understand why.

Thief, written and directed by Michael Mann, is about a thief, James Caan, who prides himself on his craft and lives by a code of action he created while serving 11 years in prison. He agrees to pull a job for someone else but is double-crossed, and he goes after what's his. That is *his* action.

Action is character; what a person does is what he is, not what he says.

So what makes a good character? Conflict? Definitely. Background? Definitely. Personality? Definitely.

But these qualities are only parts of the whole. In order to create a character we must first establish a *context* of character; that way, we can color and shade our various traits and mannerisms later.

What makes a good character? Four elements: *dramatic need, point of view, change, and attitude.*

Dramatic need is defined as what your character wants to win, gain, get, or achieve during the course of your screenplay.

What is your character's dramatic need? In *Tootsie,* written by Larry Gelbart and Murray Schisgal (and an uncredited Elaine May), Dustin Hoffman plays a talented but struggling actor, Michael Dorsey, who poses as a woman to get a lucrative role on a daytime TV soap opera. That is his dramatic need. When he falls in love with an actress (Jessica Lange), his need is to leave the role so he can win her love.

In *The Hustler,* Fast Eddie's dramatic need is to beat Minnesota Fats and win ten thousand dollars in one night.

Once you establish your character's dramatic need you can create obstacles to that need, and then your story becomes your character overcoming (or not overcoming) all obstacles to achieve his or her dramatic need.

Your character confronting obstacles to his or her dramatic need generates conflict, and conflict is essential to your story line. Drama *is* conflict.

When Fast Eddie plays Minnesota Fats the first time around, he loses; pride, overconfidence, and a "losing" attitude—he drinks too much during the game—bring about his downfall and defeat. He is shamed and broke, a loser.

He leaves Charlie, his partner (Myron McCormick), and checks in at the bus station, where he meets Piper Laurie. Later he moves in with her and they become involved in a relationship. When he hustles a punk hustler in a waterfront pool hall, he winds up with two broken thumbs. He can't hold a cup of coffee or button his shirt, much less play a game of pool. He is forced to accept the fact that he is, indeed, a loser. When he realizes this, he signs up with Bert Gordon (George C. Scott) because "twenty-five percent of something is better than a hundred percent of nothing." His realization enables him to become a winner. After Piper Laurie commits suicide, Fast Eddie challenges Minnesota Fats and defeats him easily.

He has achieved his dramatic need. Knowing your character's dramatic need "holds" the elements of character in place.

Point of view—the way a character *sees* the world. A good character will always express a definite point of view.

Everyone has an individual point of view. A friend of mine is a vegetarian; that expresses his point of view. Another friend marches against nuclear arms, and she spends time and money supporting the cause. That expresses a point of view. A confrontation between the antinuke and the pronuke points of view creates conflict. During the days of the Vietnam war people were either for the war or against it; the conflict between the two divergent points of view ended up with violence in the streets.

A point of view expresses the way a person *sees* the world. Some people believe that all things are related, that in the large scheme of things there are no accidents, and everything happens for a purpose.

"You can't fight city hall" is another point of view. A person who believes he can fight city hall might be a character like the one portrayed by Paul Newman in *Absence of Malice*. You might create a character who believes everything that happens is God's will; that's another point of view.

Everyone has a point of view. In *Annie Hall,* Alvy Singer (Woody Allen) presents his point of view in the opening lines when he expresses "how I feel about life. A lot of suffering, pain, anxiety and problems—and it's all over much too quickly." He goes on to tell a joke "usually attributed to Groucho Marx, but—originally—Freud's: 'I would never belong to any club that would have someone like me for a member.' That's the key joke of my adult life in terms of my relationships with women." That's what the movie is about: his relationship with women. The film illustrates his point of view.

When you can understand and define your character's point of view you have a tool to use in creating character. Suppose you're writing about a woman whose point of view is that "good health is a function of keeping poisonous toxins out of our bodies": absolutely *no* preservatives, *no* sugar, *no* drugs, *no* alcohol, *no* caffeine, *no* white flour, and *no* salt. A woman who exercises regularly. With this point of view, she comes in conflict with someone, probably a man, who has an occasional drink, does some dope, eats sugar and salt, drinks coffee, and scoffs at her rigid life style. Their divergent points of view present a natural conflict with good visual components to weave through your screenplay. That means you can "open it up," making it more cinematic.

Every good character dramatizes a strong, well-defined point of view. Such a character is active—will "act" from his or her point of view, and not simply react.

Change. Does your character go through a change during your screenplay? If so, what is it? In *The Hustler,* Paul

Newman goes from being a loser to a winner. James Caan, in *Thief,* starts out trusting no one; then, wanting to settle down with Tuesday Weld, he pulls a job for a man who double-crosses him; he reverts back to his "old way" of living in prison where "nothin' means nothin'."

Ordinary People, written by Alvin Sargent from the novel by Judith Guest, shows Tim Hutton, the main character undergoing a major change. In the beginning he is closed off and withdrawn. By the end he's able to open up and express himself; he's able to understand the emotional dynamics of his brother's death and let go of his painful burden of guilt; he is able to reach out and ask for help from both his father and his psychiatrist, and he finds a girl he can confide in and likes to be with.

His father, played by Donald Sutherland, also undergoes change. He begins as conventional and complacent, but he learns to listen to his son, becomes tolerant and understanding, and soon questions himself, his attitudes, and his marriage. He even seeks help from his son's psychiatrist, played by Judd Hirsch. In short, he learns to question his own values, needs, and wants.

The only major character who does not change is the mother, played by Mary Tyler Moore. Described in the opening stage directions as being "graceful and controlled," she is like her refrigerator: "well stocked, and perfectly organized, with nothing out of place." She is a person who believes that appearance is everything. During the story she remains firmly in control, unbending in attitudes and beliefs, convinced she is right. By the end of the film, father and son have changed but she has not, and the family splinters apart. In the last scene, father and son are sitting on the porch after the mother has left. Her leaving brings father and son closer together.

Annie Hall changes: she is shy and dependent at the beginning, but later she sings in public, enrolls in university extension courses, and basically outgrows the Woody Allen character and leaves him for another man.

Attitude. Knowing your character's attitude allows you to add dimension to your people. A character's attitude may be positive or negative, superior or inferior, critical or naïve. Woody Allen portrays a cynic in *Annie Hall*. Jack Nicholson's comment in *Chinatown* that the Faye Dunaway character is a "phony, just like everybody else," expresses his attitude. Another expression of attitude is W. C. Fields's famous remark that "any man who hates dogs and children can't be all bad."

Think about your character's attitude: happy or sad? strong or weak? good or bad? tough or afraid? pessimist or optimist? Describe your character in terms of attitude.

What do you think your own attitude is?

If you know and can define these four elements of character—dramatic need, point of view, change, and attitude—you have the tools to create good character. Sometimes they will overlap, an attitude will emerge as a point of view, dramatic need will bring about change, and change will affect your character's attitude. If that happens, don't worry about it. Sometimes it's necessary to take something apart in order to put it back together.

The Exercise

Determine your main character. What is his or her dramatic need? What does your character want to win, gain, get, or achieve during the course of your screenplay? What is it that drives your character from beginning to end? Write it down. Define it.

Do the same with your character's point of view. How does your character *see* the world? Through rose-colored glasses, like a dreamer or idealist? Or through jaded and cynical eyes, like Woody Allen in *Annie Hall*? Know your character's point of view. Write it down. Define it.

What about change? Does your character go through any change during the screenplay? What is it? Write it down. Define it.

The same with your character's attitude. Write it down. Define it.

Think about these qualities. They are tools to help you create good character.

6

The Tools of Character

Wherein we examine the tools of creating character:

When you create your main character, you begin a process that will be with you from beginning to end. It is an evolving process, an educational experience that keeps growing, just like you keep growing and your character keeps growing. It is formative and ongoing.

There are many ways to approach writing character. Some writers think about their characters for a long period of time and then jump in and start writing. Others create an elaborate list of characterizations; some list major elements of a character's life on 3 × 5 cards, and some write extensive outlines or draw diagrams of behavior. Some use pictures from magazines and newspapers to help them *see* what their characters look like. "That's my character," I hear them say. They may tack the pictures above their work area so they can "be with" their characters. Some use actors and actresses as models for characters.

A good tool is anything that makes it easier for you to create character. Choose your own way. You can use some, all, or none of the tools mentioned here. It doesn't matter. What matters is whether or not it works. If it works, use it, if it doesn't, don't. Find your own style of creating character. It's got to work for *you*.

Character biography: A character biography traces your character's life from birth to the time your story begins. Writing it will help you to *form* the character.

What is your character's name? Where was he or she born? How old is he when the story begins? What does his father do for a living? What is her relationship with her mother? Any brothers or sisters? An only child? "Favored," or "unfavored"? What is his early life like? Is the character athletic, mischievous, serious, extrovert, introvert?

Go into your character's life: infancy, childhood, grammar school, junior high, high school, college, after college. If the character hasn't had formal schooling, know the equivalent "educational" experiences. Define the relationships your character has formed during the years before the story begins; these relationships will influence your character's actions during the course of the screenplay and may provide "incidents" you can use in flashbacks or in dialogue to reveal your character.

In *Annie Hall,* for example, after Alvy Singer (Woody Allen) has failed to persuade Annie Hall to return to him, he gets into his car, jams it in reverse, and slams into a parked car. He puts it in forward and rams into another car; he throws it back in reverse, steps on the gas, and smashes right into a police car. The cop gets out of his car, approaches Alvy, and politely asks to see his driver's license. "Please don't ask me to do that," Alvy says, but the cop insists. Again, Alvy says, "Don't ask me to do that," but the cop stands firm and demands that he take his license out of his wallet. The two glare at each other, then Alvy shrugs, takes out the license, holds it up for the cop to see, tears it up, and tosses it to the wind. "I have a problem with authority," he tells the cop.

It's a very funny scene—one that might have come out of an incident in a character biography.

Actors and actresses also use the character biography to build character. One actress, auditioning with Martin Scorsese for a part in *The King of Comedy,* approached her reading by doing a character biography, then structured the scene into beginning, middle, and end. Scorsese liked her and called her back three different times, twice to audition with Robert De Niro. They both liked her, but she didn't get the part. They decided to go with a thin actress. That's show biz.

If you are having trouble getting inside your character, try writing your character biography in the first person. For example: "My name is David Hollister. I was born in Boston on the fifth of July. My father was a traveling salesman, and he was gone most of the time. I didn't understand why, but I thought I had something to do with it."

Some biographies will feel better written in the third person, others in the first. Do whatever helps you the most. The "tools" are there for you.

Define the *professional, personal,* and *private* aspects of your character. What does your main character do for a living? What is his or her relationship with the boss? Good? Bad? Feeling neglected? Taken advantage of? Underpaid? How long has your character worked at his or her present job? What is your character's relationship with his or her associates? Does he or she socialize with them?

Where did he or she begin his or her career? In the mailroom? At an executive training program?

If you don't know, who does?

The same with your character's *personal life.* Is your character single, married, widowed, divorced, or separated? If your character is married, how long and to whom? Where did they meet? Blind date? Chance? Business meeting? Is it a good marriage? A dying marriage? Describe it in a page or two.

The *private life* is what your character does when he or she is alone. What hobbies or interests does he or she have? Jogging? Exercise class? University extension courses? Cooking, woodwork, fixing up a house, painting, writing? In one of John Frankenheimer's films the main character, a detective, takes a gourmet French cooking class one night a week. It's a great touch.

Write your character's professional, personal, and private life in a page or two. Define it. It is a process that *reveals* character.

Research is another tool you can use to expand your ability in creating character. There are two kinds of research, *live* research and *textual* research.

In *live* research you interview people for ideas, thoughts, feelings, experience, and background material. Suppose you're writing a story about an auto plant and you want to know how it functions and operates; go there and talk to the people in personnel, in management, in design, and on the assembly line. Take a small cassette recorder and notepad. If you need to interview the people by phone, ask if you can record them; most of the time they'll say yes, especially if you tell them you're writing a screenplay or teleplay. Write out a list of questions you want to ask.

If you read a newspaper story and you want to talk to the people, call the paper, ask for the reporter who wrote the story, and see if you can get in touch with them. There should be no problem. Call them and ask if you can interview them, see what you can learn. A friend of mine, a well-known studio executive turned writer, wrote a story about a professional assassin. He finished the first draft and told me he wasn't satisfied with it; he asked me to read it. I did, and while the subject was good, the story was superficial, lacking in depth and dimension. I asked how much research he had done and surprised, he replied, "None." I told him it showed, and he ought to think about researching his main character before he began the rewrite.

Rolling Stone had just published an in-depth interview with a professional assassin a few weeks before, and I sent it to my friend. He called *Rolling Stone,* talked to the reporter who had done the piece, located the assassin, and arranged to meet him. My friend learned more about the world of the assassin than he ever conceived. He rewrote the script (he made an agreement with the man that if the film was made he would be hired as a special consultant at a good salary) and it wasn't long before it was optioned by a producer, then sold to a studio and made into a movie.

Research is a marvelous tool for creating character.

When I was writing a screenplay about an archeologist on a field trip, I needed some background information. I called the archeology department at UCLA and arranged to interview a graduate student who had just come back from a field trip. Then I called the Museum of Northern Arizona and spoke to the reference librarian, who sent me a complete catalogue of books, articles, films, and names of people I could talk to. It was invaluable.

Textual research is getting information from the library,

a museum, or an institution. Once you establish your subject, whether a person, place, event, or historical period, go to the library and find books written on the subject. Before deciding to read a book, look through the table of contents. Does it seem interesting? Does it apply to the area you're interested in? Leaf through a chapter or two. Is it easy to read? Have enough facts and detail? Three books should provide enough material to keep you busy for a few weeks. If necessary, go back and get other books later.

Also go to magazines and newspapers. Refer to *Readers' Guide to Periodical Literature* and to *The New York Times Index*. If you need help in finding books or periodicals, go to the reference desk of the library. Also be sure to check the bibliography in the back of each book you use. I start every project that way, whether it is an original screenplay or a documentary film.

If an expert you want to talk to is a psychiatrist, attorney, or doctor, you may have to pay a consultant fee. If the person requests a fee, *you decide* how important the information is. Do all your other research before you make the decision. Sometimes you'll find you don't need the professional's services.

A student of mine who was writing a screenplay dealing with early California felt stifled because she had never seen the San Joaquin Valley, the area she was writing about. I told her to take off for a weekend and just drive around and see what it's like. She did, found it "valuable," and completed her screenplay.

Richard Brooks, the writer-director of *In Cold Blood, The Professionals,* and *Elmer Gantry,* will spend months doing research before he writes a word. It's a wonderful tool.

So is dialogue. In my workshops and seminars, both

here and abroad, I hear people say, over and over again, "How can I improve my dialogue?" When I ask them what's wrong with it, they say, "It's weak, stilted, awkward, and phony." They might be right.

Dialogue is experiential. The more you do the easier it gets. I tell my students that when they sit down to begin writing, they'll probably write 40 to 60 pages of terrible dialogue. So what! Let it be terrible! It doesn't matter at this stage. You're going to rewrite it later, so let yourself be willing to write some awful dialogue. Most words-on-paper drafts will be this way.

"Writing is rewriting," the saying goes.

Most people get hung up on dialogue because they don't understand what it is, or what it does. They put too much importance on dialogue. They say good dialogue is "everything" in a script, and when they start writing and their dialogue doesn't fit their expectations, they become concerned. Soon they find themselves censoring their work, judging and evaluating, becoming supercritical. If they continue they will probably stop writing. All because they felt their dialogue wasn't good enough.

It's crazy.

If you're willing to write 40 to 60 pages of terrible dialogue, it will clear up by itself in the natural process of writing. By the end of the first words-on-paper draft you'll be amazed at the change. When you rewrite those pages your dialogue will improve tremendously. Some people, of course, have a better ear for dialogue than others. It's a gift few are born with. But you can develop it. You can learn to write good dialogue.

Dialogue is a function of character.

There are tools to help you write more effective dialogue. One is using a cassette recorder to tape and record people.

Tape a conversation with a friend or acquaintance. Play it back and listen to it. Notice how fragmented it is, how quickly thoughts come and go. If you want to see what "real" dialogue looks like, type it up in screenplay form. Listen for mannerisms and inflections, find the *style* of speech, the phrasing. Then think about your character speaking in those "rhythms," or in that "language."

Dustin Hoffman does this when he approaches a new part. He'll take the dialogue as written, talk to various people, and improvise scenes on tape. Then he will use whatever is most natural and effective.

Writing good dialogue is like running, playing the piano, swimming, or riding a horse. It's experiential; the more you do it the easier it gets. Never mind at first how good or how bad it is; let the creative mind emerge. Trust the process. It's larger than you are. Let your characters speak for themselves. You just keep writing. Be aware of any judgments or evaluations you're making, and don't let them *influence* you. Easier said then done, of course. Let yourself go! Write terrible dialogue! Don't get locked in to writing perfect dialogue from page one.

One of my students was writing a screenplay she had been thinking about for years. She had a readable and very elegant prose style, and when she wrote dialogue, it was beautiful. It *read* beautifully; every sentence clear and concise, every idea complete in thought and execution.

But it was terrible dialogue!

People don't talk in clear and elegant prose. People talk in fragments, run-on sentences, incomplete thoughts, changing mood and subject with the blink of an eye. Just listen to people. You'll hear everything; you'll get a whole new perspective on how people talk. Dialogue is not beautiful prose or iambic pentameter.

Good, effective dialogue will move the story forward and keep the reader turning pages. Which is the screenwriter's job: a screenplay is a reading experience before it becomes a visual one.

What does dialogue do? What is its function?

First, dialogue moves the story forward.

Second, dialogue communicates facts and information to the reader or audience.

Third, dialogue reveals character. A character will talk about himself, or other people will talk about him. Henry James had a theory, which he called the theory of illumination, that the main character occupies the center of a circle, surrounded by other characters. Each time a character interacts with the main character, he or she "illuminates" aspects of the main character, like turning on a lamp in a darkened room. Dialogue illuminates; it *reveals* something about character.

Exposition is usually achieved through dialogue; characters will talk about what has happened in order to establish the story line. Too much exposition becomes trite and mundane. You really don't need much of it. Just enough to set up the story; one scene probably, as in *Raiders of the Lost Ark*. Or visually, as in *Ordinary People*.

There are other ways to do it: a still photograph with voice-over narration "exposes" something about the character. Woody Allen does this in *Annie Hall* where he shows us what it's like growing up under a roller coaster. "Maybe that accounts for my personality," he says, "which is a little nervous I think." In Alain Resnais's film *Mon Oncle d'Amérique,* the writer, Jean Gruault, shows us pictures of the main character growing up, and has the main character talking about his early years. It is a visual way of revealing character.

Fourth, dialogue establishes relationships between characters. If you establish your main character's point of view, you can use dialogue to create an equal and opposite point of view to generate conflict and keep your story moving forward.

Dialogue also comments on the action. In *The Hustler,* when Fast Eddie (Paul Newman) first enters Ames Pool Hall and tries to hustle Big John, the big man replies, "I don't never hustle people who walk into poolrooms with leather satchels. Don't try to hustle me." In one line the relationship is established between Fast Eddie and the regulars.

Dialogue also connects scenes. You can end a scene with a character saying something, then cut to a new scene with another character continuing the dialogue. For example, you may want to write a montage sequence—a series of different shots—having your character speak as she is shopping, talking with her attorney, lounging by a pool, putting on makeup, getting into a taxi, and arriving at the opera, where she meets her husband, lover, friend, or acquaintance, and the dialogue continues as if it's one scene.

Dialogue ties your script together and makes a very effective cinematic tool. It is just one of the many tools you can use to expand and enlarge your character.

To create characters, you must "learn to know them, and this process of making their acquaintance is slow and painful. I make, as a rule, three casts of my dramas, which differ considerably from each other in characteristics, not in treatment. When I first settle down to work out my material, I feel as if I have to get to know my characters on a railroad journey. The first acquaintance is struck up and we have chatted about this and that. When I write it down again, I already have everything much more clearly, and I know the people as if I had stayed with them for a month at a hotel. I have grasped the leading points of their character, and their little peculiarities." Henrik Ibsen wrote that.

The Exercise

Write character biographies for two or three of your main characters. Focus first on their early years. Where and when was each character born? What did his father and mother do for a living? What is his relationship with his parents? Does he or she have any brothers or sisters? What's the relationship—friendly and supportive or angry and combative?

Define the other relationships the character has formed with people. Remember the theory of illumination: every character sheds light on your main character.

What about grammar school? A good student? What did he or she hope to be as an adult? Did he or she have many friends? Introverted or extroverted?

Go into the high school years. Was the character in any clubs? Did he or she socialize or date heavily? Belong to a gang or social club? Was the character good in athletics? Who was the first boyfriend or girlfriend? Some people "peak" in high school; is your character like this?

If the character went to college, which one? What did he or she major in? Did the character change in any way? Become politically active? A revolutionary? A serious student? Discover alcohol, turn gay? How did college affect his or her life?

What about after college? Did the character graduate?

When? If the character didn't go to college, what did he or she do? Get a job? Doing what? Get drafted? Serve in Vietnam? Travel? What about marriage and other important relationships?

Have a character biography covering each character's life up to the time your story begins.

Write three to five pages on your main character and the same for two of the other major characters. Think about the character for a few days, then set aside a period when you can work two or three hours without interruption. It may help to lower the lights or turn on soft music. When you're comfortable, start "throwing down" your thoughts, ideas, and feelings about the character. Just let it come out. Don't worry about grammar, punctuation, spelling, or bad writing. Just get your thoughts down on paper, and don't worry about anything else. You're not going to show these pages to anyone; it's only a tool for you to use while you discover your characters, to "get to know them." You may later want to include part of the character bio in your screenplay. Fine. But for now, just get your character down on paper. Free-associate. Let go; let your character discover himself or herself.

The character biography is a *process* that reveals character. It allows you to "find the voice of your character." It's like the magician pulling handkerchiefs out of his sleeve. He pulls one out, then another, then another, then another and another and another and another. We expect a lot of handkerchiefs, but when they keep coming it goes on beyond our expectations. They just keep coming out, yards and yards and yards of handkerchiefs.

What you put down on paper now paves the way for what follows. Just start writing, don't stop, or get in the way of the process. If you write 10 pages, don't rewrite it and cut it to five, because you'll lose the spontaneity.

When I do a character biography I usually end up with something like 27 pages. I start with the grandparents, then move into the parents, then into the character. I might even use past lives and astrological information.

Do the same with the professional, personal, and private lives of your character. Write a page or two about what your character does for a living. What is the relationship between your character and the people he or she works with? On good terms with the boss? Coworkers? Having an affair on the side? What is his or her goal in the company? Define it.

Do the same with the personal aspect of his or her life. Define the relationships. The same with the private aspect, the hobbies, interests, and desires. Go into your character's life and write a "day in the life"; what he or she does from the moment he gets out of bed till he goes to sleep at night. Write it in a page or two. If you need to write more, write more. If you can do it in less, do it in less.

If you discover any areas in a character's life that you feel unsure or insecure about, write it in a page or two. Just free-associate. The relationship between you and your characters is like the relationship between best friends. You decide what you need then define it.

If you don't know whether you should write it or not, write it! It's *your* script, *your* story, *your* characters, *your* dramatic choices.

When you have completed your assignment, you will know your characters as if you "had stayed with them for a month at a hotel."

And that's what it's all about.

7

The Visual Dynamics of Character

Wherein we illustrate ways to reveal your character visually:

In the English film *The Long Good Friday,* written by Barrie Keeffe, Bob Hoskins portrays an English gangster seeking to build a giant, international gaming resort in a run-down section of London's waterfront. Hoping to raise money from some American mobsters, Hoskins suddenly learns someone wants to stop the operation. A key assistant is killed in the shower; another is blown up leaving church services on Sunday; and just before the crucial meeting with the Americans the restaurant is blown to smithereens.

Hoskins is stunned. Who is doing this? And more important, why?

He goes on a rampage and combs the underworld trying to find the reasons why and the people responsible. He learns his most trusted assistant is directly involved in the plot and, in a fit of rage, kills him on board his yacht. When he leaves there's blood splattered all over him.

He returns to his luxurious flat, and the first thing he

does is take a shower. It is a revealing moment. We see him standing underneath the shower, soaking in its warmth. The camera lingers on him, and we see him naked and alone, trying to "wash away" the anger, rage, and, betrayal he feels. The shower is a visual metaphor.

As we watch Hoskins, we can feel his character's sadness and isolation; who hates this little man so much they would do this? The water cascading over him is a foreshadowing of the cleansing that will occur later that night in preparation for his own death.

The shower is a wonderful cinematic moment. It works on all levels, and visually expands our knowledge and understanding of the main character. Such scenes comprise the visual dynamics of character.

This technique is not new of course. After Macbeth murders Duncan in *Macbeth,* he tries to wash the blood off his hands:

> Will all great Neptune's ocean wash this blood
> Clean from my hand? No, this my hand will rather
> The multitudinous seas incarnadine,
> Making the green one red.

Film is a visual medium—*moving pictures*—and a screenplay is a story *told* in pictures. In a good screenplay you write your story in pictures so we can *see* the story on the page.

There is a big difference between film and television. The television screen is small, and the very form of the medium inhibits you from active participation as a viewer. We don't "see" television, we "watch" it. Furthermore, TV programs are usually geared toward the commercial, not structured according to the dramatic needs and demands of the story. When you write for television, you must be aware there is a commercial break every 10–12 minutes, and you must structure your story accordingly. (In a TV movie there are usually seven to nine commercial breaks; each act does *not* correspond to a commercial break.)

Because we *watch* television (that is we "look at" it) television is a "talking medium." A friend of mine, formerly head of the literary affairs department of a major TV company, told me that "television is a radio show with pictures." That's an accurate appraisal. Take a look at any Movie of the Week, or even a giant TV spectacular miniseries like *The Winds of War*, and you'll find that the main characters talk about their feelings, about what they want, or about what they need to do. Talking heads. They describe how they feel in *words*; it is not shown in *pictures*. Watch a TV show and see whether they "talk" the story or "show" it. (There are exceptions, of course, like the TV movie *James Dean,* written by William Bast.)

In film you "show" your story: you tell it in pictures. Knowing what visual dynamics are available to you enlarges your ability to see the relationship between story and picture. The dynamics of film are visual. Visual action *reveals* character.

Think about it. Action *is* character. What a person does is what he is, not what he says.

Thief, written and directed by Michael Mann, provides an excellent example. In the robbery that opens the film—a 10-minute sequence with no dialogue at all—we learn several things about the main character, Frank. First, he is an absolute master at what he does. He breaks through a thick bank vault with a specially designed blowtorch, then rifles through drawers of diamonds to take only the highest grade, uncut gems, and throws the other stuff on the floor.

When the job is complete, he joins his companion, walks out, gets into his getaway car, and drives slowly through the empty streets. He pulls into an empty garage, drives the car inside, locks the door, and throws the key away; the two men get into separate cars and disappear into the night. It is a masterful sequence, mastery being a thing well done.

When Frank tells Jessie (Tuesday Weld) who he is and what he does, we know all we need to know about him.

> FRANK
> What do you think I do? I
> wear 150 dollar slacks, silk
> shirts, 800 dollar suits,
> a gold watch and a perfect
> D-flawless, three-karat ring . . .
>> (pause)
> I change cars like other
> guys change shoes.
>> (Jessie looks at him)
> Hey, baby; I am a *thief*. I
> been in *prison*.

Film must convey things about character. That's why a visual dynamic is so important. Frank is a "loner," an ex-con, who wants a "normal" life: wife, family, home, two cars in the garage. He shows Jessie a collage he carries around with him. "A house with a Cadillac glued to the front. Bits and pieces of trees drawn in. A small baby from a Gerber Foods ad. A woman staring at us. Writing. Okla's face (Willie Nelson). Everything is creased and ripping a little bit.'' The pictures on the collage reveal his dramatic need, the force that drives him through the entire film. And it is the robbery that *reveals* his character.

What are the visual dynamics you can use to reveal character?

First, *physical description:* you can briefly describe your character (heavy set, chain-smokes, in his early 40's); describe the house (large and ornate); the car (fancy, late model); or the dress (elegant) of your character. Do not be specific. Be general. You don't need more than four sentences to describe your character: he lives in a ''chrome and glass apartment with modern paintings on the walls''; or she lives in a ''simple apartment, rustic in style, tasteful in decoration.'' That tells us everything we need to know about the character *visually*.

In the script of *The Wild Bunch,* Pike Bishop (William Holden) is described as a ''not unhandsome, leather-faced man in his early 40's. A thoughtful, self-educated top gun with a penchant for violence who is afraid of nothing— except the changes in himself and those around him.''

That's good character description. Brief, lucid, and to the point.

If your character drives a late-model car or an old clunker, *don't* specify year, make, model, or color. If your character dresses fashionably, don't specify *what* she is wearing. Let the costume designer and the set decorator do their job.

Setting can also reveal character. In *The Hustler,* when Paul Newman loses to Minnesota Fats, he leaves his partner and heads to the only place open that time of night, the bus station. A bus station is a place where people come and go, arrive and depart—a place of transition. Fast

Eddie, with nowhere to go, no aim, no purpose, no money—he is in a state of transition.

In the same movie, Piper Laurie plays a character with a physical deformity (she walks with a limp). The deformity represents her state of mind: She is an emotional cripple. She drinks too much, feels sorry for herself, can't handle it when Fast Eddie leaves for Kentucky. At the end of the film, she stares at herself drunkenly in the mirror, writes "crippled, perverted, twisted," and commits suicide. She is, indeed, a cripple, a casualty of self-pity. Fast Eddie changes from a loser to a winner with her help; he changes, she does not. A physical condition is a good visual dynamic that reveals character.

Sam Peckinpah and Walon Green, who wrote *The Wild Bunch,* describe Pike Bishop as "walking with a limp, always slightly in pain." He is a cripple, an "unchanged man living in a changing time."

In *Little Fauss and Big Halsy,* by Charles Eastman, Robert Redford has a long scar running up the middle of his back, and during the course of the movie we learn he has "no backbone." The scar becomes a physical manifestation of an emotional state.

Show things about your character. In Renoir's masterpiece, *La Grande Illusion,* Erich von Stroheim plays an aristocratic German officer during World War I in charge of a prison camp. In one memorable scene, von Stroheim carefully tends a single flower on his windowsill, the only spot of color in a dismal surrounding, he explains.

Another key to writing a successful screenplay is the dynamic interaction between sound and picture. They are two separate systems in the filmmaking process. When a screenplay is filmed, the picture and dialogue tracks are assembled in sequence, then edited into roughcut, then polished into a fine cut, then "locked"; nothing in the picture can be changed. Then the various sound tracks, music effects, maybe 15 or 20 individual tracks are cut, edited, and finally "locked." In the recording studio, the picture and the sound tracks are "dubbed"—"married" into a single strip of film. This is a "first answer print." It goes through many more stages before it is finally released.

When I was writing and producing television documentaries for David L. Wolper, we experimented freely. Jack Haley, Jr., Marshall Flaum, Alan Landsburg, and Mel Stuart were always searching for new ways to make film. At that time, in the early sixties, Wolper Productions was a veritable crucible of talent. William Friedkin, one of the finest filmmakers in Hollywood; Terry Sanders, who did *Word into Image* and *A Time Out of War*; Bud Smith, an exceptional film editor who cuts most of Friedkin's films and who later did *Flashdance,* and was supervising film editor on *Personal Best* (all the slow motion athletic events were directly the result of Wolper shows); Walon Green, who cowrote *The Wild Bunch, Sorcerer,* and *The Border*; David Seltzer, who wrote *The Omen,* and *The Hellstrom Chronicle;* James Brooks, who revolutionized the situation comedy with Allan Burns in *The Mary Tyler Moore Show* and all its spinoffs and won academy awards for "Terms of Endearment"; and Nick Noxon and Irwin Rosten, who did all the *National Geographic* shows from 1975 to '82, were just a few of the people working there at that time.

We had a "rule" when we did our shows (*Hollywood and the Stars; Hollywood, the Golden Years; Four Days in November,* the Biography Series, and hundreds more); it was very simple: "never tell people what they're seeing." Since we made documentaries, we used newsreel footage, stills, home movies, anything we could find to tell our stories with a voice-over narration; or we recreated a scene to bridge a sequence; we even used direct recreation of dialogue. What Woody Allen did in *Zelig* we did in documentaries.

"Don't say what you show" was a simple yet effective device that allowed us to expand the dimensions of our subject. If we showed an Army parade, for example, and our subject was Harry Truman, we would have the narrator tell about Truman's running a haberdashery shop while he dreamed of enlisting in the First World War. In that way, we expanded the viewer's knowledge of the character. What was said had nothing to do with what was shown.

You can use the sound track and the picture track to complement each other and broaden your story and character. It is a visual dynamic.

Voice-over is a very effective cinematic device. A good example is the opening of *Apocalypse Now,* written by John Milius and Francis Ford Coppola. As the film opens, we *hear* the sound of helicopters in the distance and *see* the bright blaze of napalm exploding in the jungle; on the sound track we hear Jim Morrison and The Doors singing "The End." Slowly we descend into Martin Sheen's nightmare. We *hear* his voice-over narration telling us he's "in Saigon, searching for a mission. When I was on R&R back home I wanted to be back in Saigon. When I'm in Saigon, I want to be back home on R&R." That's film! Sound and picture fused together to create a larger-than-life experience.

In Alain Resnais's *Mon Oncle d'Amérique,* written by Jean Gruault, we see snapshots in a photograph album of the main character at ages, 5, 12, 19, and 25, and hear the character commenting voice-over about what he was like growing up. It is a sequence that visually expands our understanding of character.

In *Frances* the first thing we see are early photographs of Frances Farmer (Jessica Lange), and we hear her in voice-over as she is writing in her diary. We know a lot about her from the beginning.

In *The Year of Living Dangerously,* Billy Kwan (played by Linda Hunt) keeps files on friends and associates, and as we *see* him typing in his small bungalow, we *hear* his thoughts, feelings, and observations about the person he is writing about and *see* a still photograph. We learn about the character in a *visual* way.

Still photographs, scrapbooks, photo albums, newspaper headlines, and other mementos can create this kind of visual dynamic. Show one thing and talk about another.

Five Easy Pieces (written by Adrien Joyce), one of the best American films of the last two decades, has a marvelous scene that illustrates a visual dynamic of character. Jack Nicholson, a shit-kicking oil worker, learns his father has suffered a stroke and decides he must return home to Seattle. We have seen him with his oil field buddies, and know he is involved with a not-too-bright waitress, played by Karen Black. We assume he comes from a working-class background.

When he arrives home, we learn about his upper-middle-class background, which visually collides with what we have seen in Act I. It says a lot about his character; he doesn't like who he is.

The director (Bob Rafelson) shows us Nicholson looking at a group of family pictures hanging on the wall, and we see several shots of him as a child. As he studies the stills, we can study his face, tense and tight, a striking contrast between what was and what is.

If you want to write a scene or sequence showing a series of scenes or stills with dialogue voice-over, write the dialogue first without regard to the visuals. Make sure you tighten the dialogue as much as possible.

Then, on another page, indicate the still pictures or scenes in the order in which you want to use them. If you're using only stills, describe each still on a 3 × 5 card, then play around with the visual progression. *Choose carefully. Don't use more than four or five stills in the sequence.*

When dialogue and still progression are written, take a third sheet and intercut them. Now polish the scene, weaving word and image together, tightly. If it doesn't work, find another still or stills to make it work; smooth out the transitions until the sequence flows.

Robert Towne, in an interview, commented that television teaches you to write badly because you have to write about what you're seeing; you have to write about "the problem." You have no chance to create any subtext of a scene. Subtext is what happens below the surface of the scene; thoughts, feelings, judgments—what is *unsaid* rather than *said*. We've all had the experience partaking in a conversation in which what is said has nothing to do with how the people feel. At a party, when you begin a conversation with someone you're attracted to, what are you *really* talking about?

There is a wonderful example of this in *Annie Hall*.

ALVY
(gestures to photos on the wall)

> . . . They're wonderful, you know.
> They have . . . they have, uh . . . a
> . . . a quality.

Title: You are a great-looking girl.

ANNIE
. . . I would like to take a serious
photography course soon.

Title: He probably thinks I'm a yo-yo.

ALVY
Photography's interesting, 'cause, you
know, it's—it's a new art form, and a,
uh, a set of aesthetic criteria haven't
emerged yet.

Title: I wonder what she looks like naked?

The "flashback" is a visual dynamic intercutting a scene
in the present with a scene from the past, like the drowning sequence in *Ordinary People,* the rape sequence in
Midnight Cowboy, or the memories of Lillian Hellman in
Julia. Flashbacks can be a fragment of a scene, a whole
scene, or most of the movie. *Little Big Man* opens with
Dustin Hoffman giving an interview to a reporter when he
is 102 years old, and then we *see* the story he tells.

Aspiring screenwriters have a tendency to use flashbacks when they're not needed, and it's become an over-
used device. As Tony Bill has remarked, "When I read a
flashback in a screenplay, I know the writer's usually in
trouble." A flashback can expand your story if you are
inventive, but sometimes it can get in your way.

The Wild Bunch, was originally written with several
long flashbacks showing the relationship between Robert
Ryan and William Holden when they were in prison. But
the flashbacks slowed down the story, and after the first

few previews they were cut. The film became much better: lean, clean, and tight.

If you do use flashbacks, be careful. The easiest way to show something is not always the best way. If your character says "I broke my leg skiing," a flashback sequence of your character skiing, falling, rolling, sliding, and plunging down a mountain may be a good action sequence, but it probably will do nothing to move the action of your story forward. Film deals in *present* time unless you need to reveal something that is essential; don't *impede* the flow of action.

If you use a flashback, structure it carefully, like Alvin Sargent did in *Ordinary People*. First we see a few shots of a boat sinking in a storm and someone drowning; then we see Tim Hutton waking up. His nightmare was only a fragment of the boating accident. The same image is used over and over again, building tension visually, leading to the plot point at the end of Act II. After his friend's suicide, Tim Hutton calls his psychiatrist in the middle of the night and relives the boating accident that took the life of his older brother; Plot Point II is the flashback showing what really happened.

It's an excellent example of effective use of flashback in a screenplay. If you employ this tool, design it carefully, structure it and weave it into the action so it becomes an integral part of the screenplay, like an ice cube and water.

There are other visual ways to expand character. You can have your character write in a journal or diary; flashforwards can also be used, and special effects, as in *Star Wars,* and *Return of the Jedi.* Silence and sound effects can be used to heighten and illuminate the action.

Can you think of anything else you might be able to use? Write it down. Use it.

You are telling your story in pictures, so find the best way to illustrate your character visually.

The Exercise

Think about the visual dynamics of character. What do you see your character ''doing'' during the course of your screenplay? Do you see him or her writing in a diary or journal? Can you use a narrator for your story, as Terry Malick does in *Days of Heaven*? If this doesn't work for your story, find another way.

What about flashbacks? Are they necessary? Can you use newsreels or home movies, like Sydney Pollack does in *Absence of Malice*? He opens the film with the FBI ''movies'' of Paul Newman at his father's funeral. It is lean and tight, and it works.

See how your story lends itself to any visual dynamics. Think in terms of pictures, about how you can visually expand the action of your character.

Action *is* character.

Let your story *tell you* what you can or can't use.

part two: **EXECUTION**

8

Structuring Act I

Wherein we "start" the words-on-paper:

We've done our preparation: we've taken a three-sentence idea and expanded it into a four-page treatment focusing on dramatic structure, ending, beginning, Plot Point I, and Plot Point II. We've done our character biographies, defining dramatic needs and points of view, and have done whatever research is needed.

Now what? What's the next step in the screenwriting process?

Structuring Act One.

Act I is a unit, or block, of dramatic action. It begins on page one and goes to the plot point at the end of Act I. It is 30 pages long, and held together with the dramatic context known as the setup.

In this first 30-page unit you must set up your story, your characters, your situation. Everything in Act I relates to the setup.

Your story must be established immediately, within the first 10 pages. It is the dramatic context that holds everything together, *holds* the content, or action, in place.

The opening of *Body Heat* is an excellent example. The first words on the first page describe the entire film.

"Flames in a night sky." Ned Racine (William Hurt) is established as a careless, shoddy, incompetent attorney searching for a quick score.

In the second 10 pages, after he meets Matty Walker, we see him searching for her, and in the third 10 pages he finds her. They have a drink and she agrees to let him come back to her place (nothing's going to happen, she insists) to see "her collection of wind chimes." When it's time to leave he pauses, reluctant. He wants her. He walks to his car and stands staring at Matty through the large windows that border the front door. The music swells, lust rages through him, and unable to stop, he moves toward her. He charges right through the glass, takes her in his arms, and in the throes of passion makes love to her on the floor.

That's Act I, a 30-page unit of dramatic action.

Lawrence Kasdan, the screenwriter and director of *Body Heat*, has set up the story from the beginning, from the very first words of the screenplay, "Flames in a night sky." *Body Heat* is the story of lust, passion, and betrayal, and everything in the first 30 pages establishes, or sets up, Ned Racine.

Act I sets up your story; therefore you must "design" it carefully. The first thing you have to establish is the dramatic context. What holds the act together? What do you need to set up your story? Is it the "marriage" of Jill Clayburgh in *An Unmarried Woman*? Is it establishing that E.T. has missed the spaceship home and is now "stuck" on an alien planet? Are you setting up a strong-willed individual like Gandhi? Are you setting up and establishing a new reporter arriving in a foreign country, like Mel Gibson in *The Year of Living Dangerously*?

Decide what you want to show. Define it. Describe it.

Now you're ready to structure the first act. Take some 3 × 5 cards and start laying out your story, one card per scene. Where does your story open? At the office on Monday morning? With your character pulling a robbery, as in *Thief*?

Write the opening scene on a 3 × 5 card; not the entire scene, just the idea of the scene. *Use only a few words per card, no more than five or ten.* Then write the next scene on another card, again using no more than a few words. For example, if your story is about an American journalist in Paris on assignment who meets a young French woman and falls in love, your first card might read, "arrives in Paris." The second card, "checks into hotel; calls wife back home"; third card, "meets editor"; fourth card, "briefed on his subject and assignment"; fifth card, "sees the subject at an official reception; does not talk to him"; sixth card, "arrives at the Ministry of Culture"; seventh card, "interviews subject"; and so on, scene by scene, card by card, leading to the plot point at the end of Act I when he "meets the young woman" he falls in love with.

You can do it all in 14 cards. Lay the cards out one by one, from the first scene to the plot point at the end of Act I. Free-associate. What happens? What happens next? You may want to add a few words of dialogue on the cards to help smooth out the flow of the story line. Don't get *too* specific; be vague and general, as you lay out the action in broad strokes.

If you want an action sequence, simply write "chase sequence," or "robbery sequence," or "fight sequence," or "race sequence"; you don't need any more than that at this point.

Sometimes people will fill out both sides of a 3 × 5 card, writing extensive description and dialogue. When they begin writing their screenplay, they simply transfer what's on the cards to the page. It doesn't work. When you do the cards, do the cards. When you write the screenplay, write the screenplay.

Screenwriting is a *process*; it changes constantly; it can't be too defined, or restructured. It must be left free and open, unlimited.

Do the cards for Act I. Free-associate. Lay down your thoughts quickly. You can always change them later. When you finish (it will usually take a few hours), read the cards over and over again, smoothing out the words to read easily. Change any card you want; shuffle the cards if necessary to make the story line read better. Each card moves the story forward, step by step, scene by scene.

When you've completed structuring Act I, you're ready to define the *back story*.

The *back story* is what happens to your main character a day, a week, or an hour before your story begins.

What happens? What's the first scene you're going to write? Where does it take place? When does it occur? And most important, where is your character coming from?

Many times, people start writing a screenplay and don't know where they're going. They'll spend 10 or 12 pages just searching for their story, not knowing what's wrong, only that it's "boring and trite." That's the way they muddle through the first few scenes.

As a writer, you've got to grab your reader immediately, from page one, just like *Body Heat*. You don't have time to find out what your first scene is about; *you've* got to *know* what it's about.

If you don't know, who does?

The back story helps you leap into your script, generating strong dramatic tension immediately. What happens to *your* character, a day, a week, or an hour before the story begins?

Suppose your script opens with your main character arriving at work on Monday morning. The back story might be that on Friday afternoon your character went to his or her boss and asked for a raise and the boss said no.

Your character goes home and suffers through a long weekend. You open your script on Monday morning as your character arrives at work. Imagine him getting off the elevator: Is he grim and tight-lipped, or jocular, noncaring?

See what the back story does? It allows you to enter the action from page one, word one. You know the purpose of the opening scene immediately, you don't have to "search" for it, or try and figure out what's going to happen in it. That scene is always the most difficult to write. With the back story you can achieve maximum dramatic value from page one.

One of my students was writing a story about a woman stage director preparing her first theatrical production off-Broadway. She was having difficulty defining the emotional state of the main character and didn't know where or how to open her story. Every time she sketched an opening, it was wordy, filled with unnecessary dialogue and exposition.

She didn't know what to do. I told her to write up a back story and include something in the main character's marriage that might influence the action of the play within the screenplay. Then I asked her what the story of the play was about that the main character was directing; she didn't know. Well, I said, if she didn't know, who did?

So she went home and wrote the back story and it opened up the entire screenplay. What she "found" in the back story was this: the marriage was in trouble; the main character wanted to have a child, her husband didn't; when the opportunity came for her to direct the off-Broadway play, she jumped at it. He became jealous and resentful, and the gap between the main character and her husband grew wider.

The back story takes place about three weeks before the play's opening (the opening was Plot Point I) and it's not working. Something's wrong, something's missing. Tense and frustrated, the director gets into "another argument" with her husband just before an important rehearsal. Angry and upset, she jumps into her car and takes off. As she is driving, she gets an insight into why the play isn't working, and suddenly understands what she has to do to make it work. She races to the theater to meet the actors in rehearsal.

That was the back story. So she opened her screenplay with the main character pulling into the theater parking lot, slamming on her brakes, and rushing inside to begin the rehearsal with a newfound awareness.

The back story allowed her to open her script with strong dramatic tension; to "jump" into her story with a rolling start: she didn't have to search for her story in the first few pages.

She went from not knowing how the story opened to knowing exactly what she had to do to open it dramatically, effectively, and visually. Remember, you've only got 10 pages to grab your reader.

If your screenplay has a "play within a play," like a radio show, a soap opera, a play, or a film, you must be able to describe what the story's about in a few sentences. That way you can structure a progression of the story within the story to emotionally influence the main character's dramatic need.

Do *you* know the back story of *your* screenplay?

What happens to your main character a day, a week, or an hour before your story begins?

Write it up in a few pages.

Sometimes, people tell me they like their back story so much they're going to open up their screenplay with it.

Fine.

If that happens, just write up another back story; you must always know where your character is coming from, whether you show it or not. Actors do this all the time; before an actor enters a scene he has to know where he's coming from, what the purpose of the scene is, and where he's going when the scene is over. That's just good preparation.

Do the same with the back story.

Sometimes the back story will become part of the screenplay, sometimes not. It depends on the individual script.

The Exercise

Determine the dramatic context of Act I.

Then structure the action of Act I on fourteen 3 × 5 cards. Remember, Act I is a unit of dramatic action that is 30 pages long and held together with the dramatic context known as the setup.

Lay the story out on the cards, one scene per card, using

no more than a few words on each card. Start at the beginning of your story and move through the action leading to the plot point at the end of Act I. Free-associate. You know *where* you're going, all you have to do is get there. When you've completed the cards, read them over and over again. Don't change anything until you feel the ''urge'' to. Then change a word here, a word there, to make the cards read smoothly and simply. Describe the story line in broad and general strokes.

After you've done the cards, write up the back story. Remember, it will influence the action of the first 10 pages. Look at your opening scene. Where does it take place? Describe it. Define it.

When the script opens, where is your character coming from?

Just free-associate. Lay it out, regardless of grammar or punctuation or any story holes you may have. Can you lay out the back story in terms of beginning, middle, and end? The back story can usually be written in a couple of pages, but if you need more, use them. It doesn't matter how long or how short it is. It is simply a working tool in the screenwriting process, one of the many keys to a dynamic cinematic opening.

9

The First Ten Pages

Wherein we examine the importance of the first ten pages:

During the two years that I was head of the story department at Cinemobile Systems, I read more than 2,000 screenplays and almost a hundred novels. I read so much I couldn't see straight. There was always a pile of scripts on my desk and I was always 70 scripts behind. No matter how many I read, the pile remained unchanged. Every time I thought I was caught up, my boss, Fouad Said, would walk in and tell me a new batch of submissions was coming in and that I "better hurry" if I didn't want to fall too far behind. That meant I could expect about a hundred screenplays to arrive in the next day or so.

I looked for any excuse to avoid reading a script. If a script came in with a one-page synopsis, I read the synopsis only. If the writer told me the story, when he or she submitted the script, I read the first few pages, a page or two in the middle, and the last three. If I liked the story line, or the situation, and the way it was written, I read it; if I didn't, I didn't. If I had too much to eat for lunch, or if I had too much to drink, I would lean back in my chair, read the first few pages, prop it on my lap, turn off the phones, and take a 10- or 15-minute nap.

Out of all that material, I only found 40 screenplays worth submitting to our financial partners for possible production. Out of those 40 some 37 films were made, including *Jeremiah Johnson, Alice Doesn't Live Here Anymore, The Wind and the Lion,* and *Taxi Driver.* When I began to study these scripts, I began to enlarge my understanding about the art and craft of screenwriting.

I began by asking myself what made these 40 scripts better than the other 1,960 I read, and I didn't have any answers for a long time. When I was given the opportunity of teaching a screenwriting course, I was forced to go into my own writing and reading experience for my material. I didn't know too much at the beginning; my students taught me everything.

I learned that the first thing a reader notices is the *way* the writer puts words down on the page—the *style* of the writing. The second is *what* the story is about, and *who* it is about. The third is whether the action and characters are "set up" in a strong dramatic context.

I made most of my decisions within the first 10 pages. Should I continue reading? Did I *want* to continue? What *is* the story? Who *is* the main character? What *is* the dramatic premise? What's it about? I discovered I could tell whether or not a script was working within the first 10 pages.

You've only got 10 pages to grab your reader. You better make sure these 10 pages are lean, clean, and tight.

In my eight-week screenwriting workshops, we spend the first four weeks preparing the material and the second four weeks writing it. I stress the fact that the first 10 pages of the screenplay are the most important. When you sit down to write the opening pages, you must think in terms of writing a separate unit of dramatic or comedic action. You have to design those first 10 pages with skill, economy, and imagination.

You've got to grab the reader's attention immediately. You don't have time to wander, searching for your story. If you haven't involved your reader in the story within the first 10 pages, you've lost him. You must set up three major elements in those first 10 pages:

Number one: Who is the main character—*who* is your story about? Number two: what is the dramatic premise—*what* is your story about? Number three: what is the dramatic situation—what are the *circumstances* surrounding the action?

These three things must be introduced within the first 10 pages. Once you determine how you're going to incorporate these three elements, you can design and structure the first 10 pages as a unit, or block, of dramatic action.

What is your opening scene? Where does it take place? Is it a dialogue scene or a series of shots? Do you want your screenplay to begin by evoking a mood, like *Tender Mercies*? Or by establishing the texture of a time and place, like *Gandhi*? Maybe you want it to open with an exciting action sequence like *Return of the Jedi*. Do you want the opening to be loud and noisy or tense and suspenseful? A car driving through deserted city streets at night, or a man strolling through a crowded park on a Sunday afternoon?

What is your main character doing? Where is he or she coming from? Going to? Think about it. Define it. Articulate it. Structure it.

Will you be able to establish the dramatic premise in the first scene? Or are you going to do it in the fifth scene? Is the scene clear enough in your mind to dramatize it? If your opening is an action sequence (like the robbery in *Thief*), structure the action into beginning, middle, and end. Then choose the most exciting part and start there. Grab your reader's attention. Do you see the first scene in close shots or in a master shot (which shows the widest field of vision)? Look for visual impressions that will make the scene work.

You have 10 pages to grab your reader, so you better design them carefully, with skill and precision; you better know what you're writing about.

Because if you don't, who does?

Introduce your main character, establish the dramatic premise, and create the dramatic situation.

You have to set up your story line immediately. Reread the first 10 pages of *Chinatown* in Chapter 7 of *Screenplay*. You might want to reread Chapter 6, "Endings and Beginnings," as well.

The opening of *Thief* is another good example: a tense action scene—James Caan pulling a sophisticated jewel robbery. We see immediately that he is the main character and a master thief. When the fence is murdered on page 6, he wants his diamonds back, but only what's his, no more, no less. That's the dramatic premise of the film.

The main character and the dramatic premise are set up immediately. We see that James Caan owns a used car lot, and we'll learn he spent 11 years of his life in prison (the dramatic situation) and wants to marry Tuesday Weld.

In the first shot and the opening monologue of *Annie Hall,* Woody Allen says, "Annie and I broke up and I—I still can't get my mind around that. You know, I keep sifting the pieces o' the relationship through my mind and—and examining my life and tryin' to figure out where did the screw-up come."

That's the whole film; it's told in flashback because when the movie opens the relationship is over (endings and beginnings are related, right?) and the film shows us the "pieces of relationship" beginning with Plot Point I, when Annie Hall and Alvy Singer meet on the tennis court with Michael Murphy. It's all set up in the very first page.

Body Heat opens with Ned Racine looking out the window at a distant fire while Angela, his one-night stand, gets dressed. Racine says that it was "probably one of my clients" who started the fire, and we'll learn later that one of his clients is an arsonist. On page 3 he is in court with his friend Lowenstein, the assistant county prosecutor. Racine, we learn, is an "incompetent" attorney. "The judge is irritated" because Racine has "failed to generate the semblance of a defense" and tells him "the next time you come into my courtroom I hope you've got either a better defense or a better class of client." On page 4, he is having lunch with Lowenstein and we learn that Racine is a man who's "searching for a quick score." It tells us a lot about him.

We see him in his law office on page 6, with the elderly Mrs. Singer; Racine sent her to a doctor who will not testify on her behalf, so he tells her he will find a "more understanding" doctor. "We'll sue those reckless bastards dry," he adds.

On page 7 it's night and he's bored. He has a drink at the bar, then wanders over to the beach-front bandstand. He listens to the music, then sees Matty Walker, "this extraordinary, beautiful woman," walking toward him. "She passes within a few inches of him . . . Racine's body sways a moment as she goes by as though buffeted by some force.''

He follows her, and during their conversation she tells him she is a married woman; he replies that she should have said "I'm a *happily* married woman." She sizes him up and says, "You're not too smart, are you?" Then, as an afterthought, "I like that in a man."

He remarks that she looks "well tended," then adds, "I need tending, but only for the night." Racine's the type of person, Lowenstein says later, "whose dick gets him into trouble." When Matty spills a cherry Sno-Kone on her blouse, he gets some paper towels, but when he returns she's gone, vanished into the night.

That's the first 10 pages of *Body Heat*—perfect illustration of a well-designed opening.

The Exercise

You've done your preparation. You've clarified your story line, done your character work, structured the first act on 3 × 5 cards, written the back story, designed the first 10 pages. You're ready to start writing.

The first 10 pages are going to be the most difficult; you'll probably experience confusion, doubt, and uncertainty. Never mind. Just sit down and do it.

Don't think about it, just do it. Jump in. Trust the *process,* it's larger than you, a truly marvelous and mysterious creative experience. No matter what the results, good or bad, negative or positive, "true art," as Jean Renoir once told me, "is in the *doing.*"

The very worst that can happen is that you write a

terrible screenplay. So what? If it's that bad, just throw it away! You're not obligated to show it to anyone.

Don't worry about judgments and evaluations. You *will* have them. You won't know how good or bad your script is until after you're written it. That means three drafts of the "first draft" screenplay: the words-on-paper draft, the making-change-and-bringing-it-to-length draft, the final-polish draft, where you may rewrite each scene 10 times. It's important to remember that your script is going to change during these three drafts.

Let it change.

Just tell the story.

If you ask yourself how good or bad your first few pages are, guess what the answer is? Bad, obviously. It's boring, dull, trite, and ordinary, and you've seen it all before. That may be an accurate judgment. But who's making that judgment? You are.

Let it go. It's only a judgment; it doesn't mean anything. "The mind," Swami Muktananda said, "is a strange and funny thing. In the summer it longs for winter, and in the winter it longs for summer."

Judgment is part of the screenwriting process. Expect it. Don't let it interfere with the experience of writing. Reread Chapter 12 of *Screenplay,* "Screenplay Form," and Chapter 14, "Writing the Screenplay." Form should never get in the way of your screenwriting. It's very simple: dialogue goes in the center of the page, and the name of the person speaking is capitalized; the description, single-spaced, goes from margin to margin. Leave a lot of space on the page, never crowd it. Directions indicating where and when the action takes place are always capitalized: INT. AUDITORIUM—DAY or EXT. JOGGING TRACK —DUSK (inside of an auditorium during the day, outside on a track at dusk, respectively).

Set your left margin at 15; dialogue should be tabbed to begin on 32; character speaking (in caps) is tabbed at 40; dialogue should end about 58, and your right margin be at about 75. Adjust these to suit your own needs and typewriter.

It might help if you typed up 10 pages of a screenplay. Take any screenplay, open it at random, and simply type 10 pages. Just type the pages, familiarizing yourself with the feel of the form. If you don't have access to any screenplays, copy one of the excerpts in *Screenplay*. Just copy it off the page, word for word, shot by shot. You may find it an effective way to help start the screenwriting process.

When you start writing, just lay your story line out scene by scene, shot by shot. You may find it easier to write everything in master shots: INT. RESTAURANT or EXT. PARKING LOT. Be willing to make some mistakes. You're not going to write perfectly from page 1.

Just *tell your story*.

When I was working with Jean Renoir, he remarked that beginning a new creative project, whether it be a painting, a symphony, or a novel, is very much like going into a clothes shop and trying on a new jacket. When you try it on the first time, it doesn't look right or feel right. You take it in here, let it out there, alter it so it fits. When you try it on again, it looks all right, but it still feels a little tight under the arms. You shrug your shoulders to loosen it up a bit, and make it a little more comfortable. "But you have to wear it awhile before you get used to it," Renoir said.

It's the same principle when you're writing a screenplay. You've got to get used to it.

Give yourself a chance to write some terrible pages. Be willing to try things that may not work, to write awkward, stilted, or boring dialogue. It doesn't matter at this stage.

Sit down and write the fist 10 pages of your screenplay, focusing on your main character, the dramatic premise, and the dramatic situation.

"The longest journey," remember, "begins with the first step."

10

The Second and Third Ten Pages

Wherein we follow focus and define the story:

When I first started teaching my screenwriting workshops, my students worked very hard designing and executing the first 10 pages of their scripts. But when they moved into the second 10 pages, it was like night and day. New characters were added, elaborate action sequences conceived, gimmicks were introduced that had absolutely nothing to do with the story line at all. It was as if they worked so hard writing the first 10 pages they didn't know what to do in the second 10. They seemed "obligated" to create elaborate scenes in order to "break free" of that opening section and let loose, regardless of whether it fit the story or not.

The results were awful. All confusion and no story. The reader was lost. The story line wandered around in search of itself, going nowhere.

Nothing worked.

Act I is a unit of dramatic action that is 30 pages long and goes from page 1 to the plot point at the end of Act I. It is held together by the dramatic context known as the setup. It establishes the main character, dramatic premise, and dramatic situation. It has direction; that is, it follows a specific line of development.

In the second 10 pages you must follow the focus of your main character.

In *Chinatown* everything is set up in the first 10 pages (Chapter 7 of *Screenplay*). In the second 10 pages Jake Gittes starts the job he was hired to do: to find out who Mulwray is "having an affair with."

What does Gittes do?

He follows Mulwray from the council chambers to the Los Angeles riverbed, then trails him to the beach where water is being dumped into the ocean during the middle of a drought. He puts watches under the tires of Mulwray's car and learns that he was there until almost 3:00 A.M. The "guy's got water on the brain," he says. Pictures taken outside the Pig 'n' Whistle reveal Mulwray having a violent argument with Noah Cross (John Huston). The phone rings and Gittes learns that Mulwray has been spotted at Echo Park with "the girl."

"Jesus," Gittes says, "water again." He takes pictures of the couple, and as far as he's concerned, that's it, the case is closed.

He goes for a haircut and is surprised to see the pictures he took of Mulwray and "the girl" on the front page of *The Times* with the headline "Department of Water and Power Blows Fuse Over Chief's Love Nest."

He doesn't know how the pictures got there.

That's the second 10 pages of *Chinatown*. Action and reaction. Gittes is hired in the first 10 pages, does his job in the second 10 pages. Notice how the thread of the story weaves through the action focusing on the events leading Gittes into uncovering a major water scandal.

The "rule" of the second 10 pages is *follow the focus of your main character*.

Design the second 10 pages with as much care and efficiency as you did with Act I. Lay out your cards. Do they still apply? Do you need any new scenes, scenes you hadn't thought of before? If so, use them. Is your main character in every scene? He should be. Is your character *active*—does he or she initiate the action and respond to the premise and situation of the first 10 pages? Remember Newton's third law of motion: "For every action there is an equal and opposite reaction."

Your main character must be *active:* he or she should be making all the decisions about what to do or where to go. The first 10 pages set up your character, premise, and situation; the second 10 pages focus on your character and the dramatic premise. Your story is always moving forward with direction, a line of development.

If you want to make any changes, make the changes, *see* what happens; it may work, it may not. The worst that can happen is that you make a mistake; you'll just have to go back and do it another way—maybe even the way you originally planned. You'll know within a few pages whether the changes are working.

Add whatever you need. *Do* whatever you need to do to make the story line clear and concise.

Do not feel "obligated" to remain "true" to reality. If you're writing a story based on a real event, the tendency will be to remain true to the way things *really* happened. It doesn't work. The "reality" of the event will get in the way of the dramatic needs of your story.

I have to tell my students over and over to "let go" of the original source material and simply write what is needed for their story. One student was writing a screenplay based on a diary of a Hawaiian woman in the early 1800s whose husband contracted leprosy; the couple become outcasts, hunted down by a posse determined to eradicate them. A true story.

When my student started writing she used exact scenes and dialogue from the diary, faithfully recording authentic customs and traditions of the islanders.

It didn't work. It was boring. It had no structure, therefore no story line or direction.

We came up with some ideas for making the story more dramatic. She added new scenes that were true to the integrity of the source material. The story blossomed.

When she did the rewrite she had to change most of Act I and a good portion of Act II, but it didn't take her long. She knew exactly what she had to do to make the story work, and she did it.

The hardest thing about writing is knowing what to write.

Let go of the reality of the person, incident, or event. Find the unreality, the theatricality. This *is* a movie, remember. You must communicate the people, the story, and the events dramatically.

Reality only gets in the way. Let it go. Make up your own scenes *based* on the people, incidents, and experience.

In the third 10 pages we move up to the plot point at the end of Act I, ''an incident, episode, or event that 'hooks' into the action and spins it around into another direction.'' It occurs around page 25 or 27 and takes you into Act II. (Reread Chapter 9 of *Screenplay* for an extended discussion of the plot point.)

Ordinary People provides a good illustration of setting up the dramatic premise in the first 10 pages, following focus on the main character in the second 10 pages, and easing into the plot point at the end of Act I in the third 10 pages.

The first 10 pages set up the story: we *see* Conrad Jarrett (Tim Hutton) in choir practice: We *see* Beth (Mary Tyler Moore) in her "neat, organized, and perfect" household. We *see* Calvin, her husband (Donald Sutherland), returning home on a commuter train. It's like a Norman Rockwell painting, the "perfect" family. Except when Calvin leaves the train a friend says "Cal—we're sorry—about everything." Strange.

On page 9, Calvin asks his son, Conrad (Tim Hutton): "Have you thought about calling that doctor?"

"No," Conrad replies.

"The month's up, I think we should stick to the plan," his father continues.

"The plan was *if* I needed to call him," Conrad says.

His father backs off. "Okay, don't worry about it. Go to sleep."

Those are the first 10 pages of the script. The perfect picture of ordinary people, only something's wrong and we don't know what.

The second 10 pages begin with Conrad waking from a nightmare, "perspiring and scared." We see Conrad coming down to breakfast, and the kitchen *looks* great; everything clean and neat, French toast sizzling in the frying pan, a newspaper sprawled out in front of Calvin. It's perfect save for one thing: Conrad's not hungry. His mother, self-righteous and indignant, throws the French toast down the garbage disposal, and the father tries to placate the two unsuccessfully.

On page 12, Conrad is picked up by his "buddies," but when he enters school we see he is distant and insecure. His English teacher offers him understanding and support, and says she does not want him to feel "pressured about this report." In the next scene, page 18, Conrad calls Dr. Berger (Judd Hirsch), a psychiatrist, and says, "Dr. Crawford at Hillsboro Hospital gave me your number."

After school Conrad goes to swimming practice and we hear the coach urging him to try harder, but something is obviously bothering him. He seems preoccupied, tense. Then he has dinner with his parents. They have a polite dinner conversation, but Conrad says nothing.

That's the second 10 pages, following focus on the main character. From page 10 through page 20, Conrad is in every shot.

The next day, page 21, Conrad goes to school, suffers an anxiety attack, and leaves school. The next shot shows him standing in front of a large building, debating about whether or not to go in. He does, and meets Dr. Berger. On the next page (page 24) we learn that Conrad was in a mental hospital for four months because "I tried to off myself." He's only been out about a month. Now the conversation on page 9 between father and son about seeing a doctor becomes clear. We learn that Conrad's brother Buck drowned in a sailing accident a short time ago and that this has something to do with Conrad's mental state.

When the psychiatrist asks "What do you want to change?" Conrad replies, "I want to be in control . . . so people can quit worrying about me."

The scene with Dr. Berger is the plot point at the end of Act I. It starts on page 23 and ends on page 26.

That night, at dinner, Conrad tells his parents that he went to see Dr. Berger. His father is pleased and encouraging, while his mother is concerned and withdrawn.

That's the first 30 pages of *Ordinary People*. It sets up the entire story.

In the first 10 pages we see there *is* a problem, the second 10 pages *define* the problem, and in the third 10 pages we understand *what the problem is*. If we wanted to diagram it, it would look like this:

1st 10 pages	2nd 10 pages	3rd 10 pages
set up main character, dramatic premise, dramatic situation	follow focus on main character in school, anxious, distant we see the symptoms "the problem"	define the problem dramatize Plot Point I going to psychiatrist to learn about Buck's drowning Plot Point I, pp. 23–26

THE SETUP

That's Act I: a unit, or block, of dramatic action. It goes from page 1 to the plot point at the end of Act I. It is approximately 30 pages long, and is held together with the dramatic context known as *the setup*.

The Exercise

Lay out the 3 or 4 cards that make up the second 10 pages of your screenplay.

Follow the focus of your main character. Is he or she in every scene? Think through the action before you start writing. See where it goes.

Tell your story. Show what is necessary and needed, as in *Ordinary People*. If you're writing a scene and something really "good" happens, go with it and write it down. Don't get in the way, just let it happen. Don't save it for a later time or another scene. Write it. Anything you "save" now will probably be forgotten later. Trust the process! When you need something you'll come up with it when you need it. That's the natural law. Trust it.

Don't worry about not having enough to say! If you're working full time and writing "on the side," each 10-page unit is a good solid week's work. Think through the action for a couple of days, then sit down to write it. You'll turn out 10 pages a week. Think of writing the script in sections, in terms of units of action, and you'll feel very comfortable with what you're doing.

Writing is a day-by-day job, one scene at a time, shot by shot, sequence by sequence, act by act.

Write the second 10 pages. Don't spend too much time cleaning it up and "making it perfect." The important thing is to keep moving forward, from beginning to end. People who spend too much time making it "right" usually run out of gas about 50 to 60 pages in and shelve their material.

If you make any judgments or decisions about your writing, it will probably be negative. You'll hate it. The first words-on-paper draft is usually awful anyway, so don't worry about it. Once you get something down on paper, you can always go back and change it, clean it up, and make it better. My first draft is usually about 60 percent of what I know it can be. When I go through it a second time I'll bring it up to about 75 or 80 percent. In my polish I'll do the best I can; 90–95 percent. Some days will be better than others.

The third 10 pages lead you directly into the plot point at the end of Act I. Have you designed your "incident or event that hooks into the action and spins it around into another direction" (in this case Act II)?

Describe it. Design it. Write it. Do you need any transition scenes to ease you into Plot Point I? Are you telling your story all in dialogue, or are you using visuals with it? A screenplay is a story told in pictures, remember, so think in terms of opening up your story. Show the car leaving the building, driving down the street; show your character getting a taxi, walking into a building and stepping into the elevator. This opens up your story, and gives it visual texture. You don't want to write your script going from INT. scene to INT. scene to INT. scene. Open it up; take it outside!

Keep your pages numbered; if you ever need to refer to a page, or add an insert scene, you've got to know where you are. Act I may end up being 36 pages. So what? You'll clean it up; keep moving forward.

Just tell your story. Don't try to tell it too quickly. Some people write their whole screenplay in the first 10 pages, then have nothing left to say. Use the first words-on-paper draft as an exercise to find your voice, to find your style.

You're going to rewrite 70–80 percent of what you've written anyway. When you've completed Act II and Act III, you'll know exactly what you have to do when you start the rewrite. Don't worry about it now. Just write your pages. When you complete the third 10 pages you're ready to move into Act II.

11

The New Paradigm

Wherein we take another look at Act II:

When I first started teaching my screenwriting workshops, I structured each class into eight-week sessions. The first class focused on Act I; we spent four weeks preparing to write the screenplay, the second four weeks actually writing it. The goal of the class was to write the first 30 pages, or Act I, of the screenplay.

When we completed the first eight-week session, we took a break, then continued on into the next class. The goal in this class was to structure, design, and complete the second act.

Most of the people kept writing during the break. They didn't want to lose the discipline and creative energy they had built up during the first class. When they returned to start the second-act class and showed me the pages they had written, I was astonished. They were awful. There was no direction, no line of development, no trace of an organic story line, and almost no conflict. When it came to the second act, they were like blind men in a rainstorm: they didn't know where they were going and they were all wet.

In my own writing experience, Act II was always the most difficult material to get through, whether I was using a typewriter, a writing pad, or a computer. Sixty sheets of blank paper are a threat—and so is a blank computer screen. It's easy to go into "overwhelm"; to just "check out," or "get lost."

That's what happened to my students when they started writing the second act. They lost their overview and did not focus on telling their story.

Act II is a unit of dramatic action that begins at the plot point at the end of Act I and goes to the plot point at the end of Act II; it is 60 pages long and held together with the dramatic context known as *confrontation*.

It looks like this:

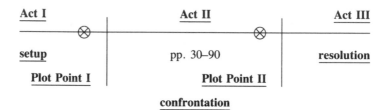

Act I	Act II	Act III
setup	pp. 30–90	resolution
Plot Point I	Plot Point II	
	confrontation	

When you're writing Act II you always have to know where you are and where you're going. Otherwise, it's easy to get lost in the maze of your own creation. As a beginning writer I simply "banged my head against the typewriter," but that was a very painful experience. As a beginning teacher, I didn't know what to do. I wanted to find a way that would make it easier for people to write Act II. I thought about it for a long time before I came up with any answers. I had to start someplace. So I began with the *paradigm*.

I began defining Act II in terms of Act I and Act III. Act II is twice the length of Acts I and III; it is a unit of action that is 60 pages long and held together with the dramatic context known as confrontation. Every time I went to a movie or read a script or taught a class, I thought about the function of Act II.

Writing is a process of asking yourself the right questions and waiting for the right answers. So I waited, and one day, while jogging, I recalled a conversation I had had with Paul Schrader (*Cat People, Taxi Driver, American Gigolo*). He said that when he writes a screenplay "something happens" about page 60.

Page 60. I hadn't thought too much about it at the time, but now I realized that page 60 is halfway through the second act.

Interesting. I wondered if it might be true in other screenplays as well. So I started rereading several screenplays.

I started with *An Unmarried Woman*. As mentioned, Act I, the setup, deals with the marriage of Jill Clayburgh. She's been married some 17 years in what she considers a very successful marriage. We see her jogging with her husband, Michael Murphy, and making love with him before he leaves for work; we see her as a mother getting her teenage daughter off to school; see her working part time in an art gallery, where she's "hustled" by Charlie the painter; we see her with her friends, and from all outward appearances she is happy and content. A good life.

Then, on page 25, her husband suddenly breaks down and blurts out, "I'm in love with another woman."

Plot Point I. From being a married woman in Act I, Jill Clayburgh becomes an unmarried woman in Act II. Almost overnight she is forced to adapt to a new life-style, another beginning. It's not easy. She has trouble being alone; she has trouble with her daughter; and she hates men. She goes into therapy. When a blind date makes a pass at her she throws him out of the taxi on the East River Drive.

In the next scene she is with her therapist, a woman, who tells her she's got to give up her anger toward men; she should experiment a little, take some risks. "I can't tell you what to do, of course," the therapist continues, "but I know what I would do."

"What?" Jill Clayburgh asks.

"I would go out and get laid."

That happens on page 60. The next scene shows her at a singles bar, where she meets Charlie the painter. She returns to his studio apartment and spends the night with him. From then on, all the way through to the end of Act II, when she meets Alan Bates, she explores her sexuality in a number of one-night stands. She doesn't want a continuing relationship. After having sex with her in the afternoon, Alan Bates tells her he wants to see her again, but she says no. "I'm experimenting. . . . I want to know how it feels to make love with a man I'm not in love with."

The scene on page 60, with the therapist, bridges the action of the first half of Act II with the second half of Act II. From page 30 to page 60 the main character is "antimen"; from page 60 to page 90—after "I would go out and get laid"—she "explores her sexuality."

Interesting.

I drew it on the *paradigm*:

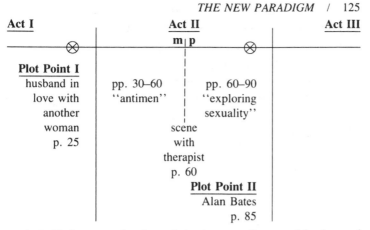

Act I	Act II		Act III
	m ⎮ p		
⊗		⊗	
Plot Point I			
husband in	pp. 30–60	pp. 60–90	
love with	"antimen"	"exploring	
another		sexuality"	
woman	scene		
p. 25	with		
	therapist		
	p. 60		
	Plot Point II		
	Alan Bates		
	p. 85		

Act II is now broken into two units, or blocks, of dramatic action. The scene with the therapist breaks it in half.

A few nights later I read *Manhattan*. When Ike (Woody Allen) and Mary (Diane Keaton) first meet, they don't like each other. She's having an affair with his best friend, Yale (Michael Murphy), a married man, and he finds her to be a pseudointellectual, a phony.

He goes his way, she goes hers. He leaves his job writing for a TV program to work on his book; he has a relationship with 17-year-old Tracy (Mariel Hemingway). Then one night quite by accident, Ike and Mary meet each other at a museum opening. And they like each other. That's Plot Point I; it happens about page 23.

They spend the night together, walking and talking about everything and nothing. Several days later, on a lonely Sunday afternoon, Mary calls Ike and they spend the afternoon together. Their friendship intensifies over the next pages and then they make love. They go from being friends to being lovers. It happens on page 60.

They create a relationship. They're with each other constantly. And then one day, out of the blue, she tells him that she thinks she's still in love with Yale; she is seeing him again. That's the plot point at the end of Act II.

When I drew it on the *paradigm*, it looked like this:

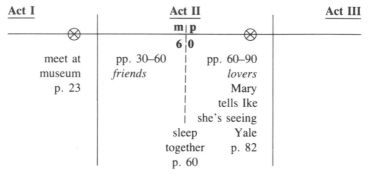

Does something always happen on page 60 that bridges the first half of Act II with the second half? Some kind of incident, episode, or event that shifts the action into another direction?

I didn't know. But I had a suspicion.

I reread *Body Heat*. The plot point at the end of Act I is the coming together of Ned Racine and Matty Walker at the foot of the stairs. In Act II they are having sex constantly, until page 43, when she casually mentions to him that she wishes her husband would die. "It's what I most want."

He agrees. "How good it would be for us if he were gone. . . . But there's no reason to think he's gonna die, so we might as well forget about it. It won't *just happen.*"

Racine's already been set up as a man who's looking for a quick score, and Matty Walker's sudden inheritance of a great deal of money is very attractive, very tempting.

He thinks about it, considers it, verifies it, analyzes it, finally knows and accepts it. "We're going to kill him. The man's gonna die for no reason but we want him dead."

He plans and executes the crime. At two o'clock one

morning he enters the house and, after a struggle, kills Matty's husband (Richard Crenna). The murder occurs on page 60. (The script was drastically changed in the cutting room.)

Once again, "something happens" about page 60 that links the first half and the second half of Act II. It can be a plot point, a sequence, a scene, a line of dialogue, a decision, some kind of incident or event that bridges the action of Act II so it continues moving forward with a specific line of development. Three scripts, three very good scripts, convinced me I was on to something.

In *Body Heat* the murder leads directly to the plot point at the end of Act II. Racine is summoned by the murdered man's attorney and told he made a mistake in changing the will. The will is now null and void. "In the state of Florida when a person dies without a will, the spouse inherits everything."

"You mean . . . it's all mine?" Matty Walker says.

Tough. At first, Racine thinks it's great, but then *he* didn't change the will, *she* did. "I hope you haven't done us in," he says.

This leads directly to Plot Point II when his best friend Lowenstein tells him that someone is out to get him. "Don't let your dick lead you into a real hassle. That lady may have just killed her husband. . . ."

It gets worse. The arsonist, Teddy, the man who gave Racine the incendiary device, tells him that his woman friend wants another incendiary device. He showed her how to operate it. Racine is shocked; he can't believe it's happening, and he stumbles through the rest of the script like a boxer out on his feet. In the end, of course, he winds up on murderers' row and she winds up in a tropical paradise talking about "how hot it is" with a beachboy.

When I put *Body Heat* on the paradigm, it looked like this:

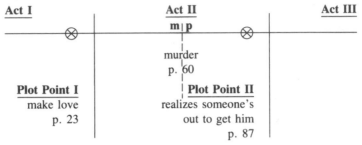

In all three examples, something definitely happens on page 60 that helps design and structure the action of Act II. That "incident or episode or event" that happens on page 60 I termed the *midpoint*, because it happens midway through the second act.

Once you establish the midpoint, Act II becomes a 60-page unit that is broken down into two basic units of dramatic action that are each 30 pages long. The first half of Act II goes from the plot point at the end of Act I to the midpoint. The second half of Act II goes from the midpoint to the plot point at the end of Act II.

The new paradigm looks like this. Everything becomes a 30-page unit of dramatic action. It works!

When I began teaching the new paradigm in my seminars and workshops, I was amazed at the results. My students suddenly had a firm grasp on Act II; they could control *it*—*it* no longer controlled them. They didn't get lost. They knew where they were going and how to get there.

The midpoint helps you design, structure, and write the second act of your screenplay.

When you're in the paradigm, you can't see the paradigm.

The Paradigm Structured

The Story:

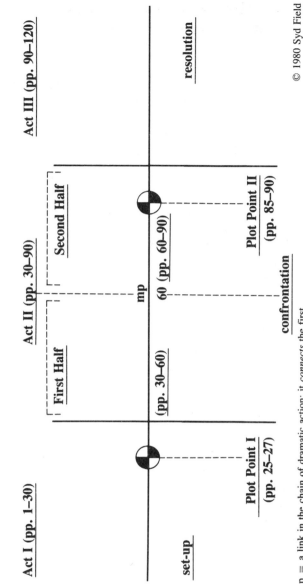

Act I (pp. 1–30)

Act II (pp. 30–90)

Act III (pp. 90–120)

First Half
(pp. 30–60)

Second Half
60 (pp. 60–90)

mp

set-up

confrontation

resolution

Plot Point I
(pp. 25–27)

Plot Point II
(pp. 85–90)

m p = a link in the chain of dramatic action; it *connects* the first half of Act II with the second half of Act II.

The Exercise

Go to a couple of movies you like and see them two or three times. When you see a movie the first time, simply enjoy it and let it wash over you.

When you see it the second time, study it. Take a pad of paper with you to take notes. Isolate and define Plot Point I and Plot Point II. See if you can find the structure of Act II. Start at Plot Point I; it occurs about 25 minutes into the film (p. 25). Check your watch if you have to.

After Plot Point I, follow the action of the main character. About 50 or 60 minutes into the film, see if you can locate the midpoint. Check your watch. When the film is over, see if your definition of the midpoint is accurate.

Why is it the midpoint? Does it link the chain of dramatic action connecting the first half of Act II with the second half of Act II?

Then see the movie again from start to finish. Check it out. You might even draw it on the *paradigm*.

12

The Midpoint

Wherein we further define the nature, function and importance of the midpoint:

When I first started teaching the concept of the midpoint, I didn't have too many explanations, or reasons, or examples of it because I didn't know too much about it.

I knew I was on to something, though I didn't know what it was, or how important it would eventually turn out to be.

About this time, two Belgian filmmakers, representatives of the Ministry of Dutch Culture in Brussels, asked me if I would teach the special screenwriting workshop in Brussels that summer (1981). During our discussion one of them asked if I had discovered anything new since the publication of *Screenplay*. I told him about the midpoint; he asked several perceptive questions, and I didn't have too many answers.

Since I was taking the film and script of *Chinatown* with me to Brussels, he asked me what the midpoint of *Chinatown* was. I didn't know. I tried to "cover" my ignorance by declaring that all I had to do was open the script to page 60. Page 60 turned out to be the scene in which Jake Gittes talks with Evelyn Mulwray in a bar soon after her husband's death. He takes an envelope out of his pocket, thanks her for the check she sent him, but adds that she's "shortchanged" him on the story. "I think you're hiding something, Mrs. Mulwray," he says. He points to the monogram on the envelope: ECM. He casually asks what the C stands for.

She stammers slightly before she answers. "C-Cross," she says.

"That's your maiden name?" he asks.

Yes.

He thinks about it for a moment, shrugs his shoulders, and changes the subject.

I put down the script, confused. "Is that the midpoint?" the filmmaker asked. I looked at him, tried to justify the scene as the midpoint, and then gave it up because it was obvious I didn't know what in the hell I was talking about. I didn't know if that was the midpoint or not, and if it was, why. I tried to laugh it off, and quickly changed the subject.

When I was preparing the workshop, I reread *Chinatown* several more times. I finally decided that the midpoint was not the scene in the bar on page 60 but the scene right afterward, in the parking lot outside, on page 63, where Gittes tells Mrs. Mulwray that her husband "was murdered, in case you're interested . . . and somebody's dumping thousands of gallons of water out of the city reservoirs when we're supposedly in the middle of a drought . . . and I goddamn near lost my nose! And I like it. I like breathing through it. And I still think you're hiding something."

As far as I was concerned that was "it." I took film and script to Brussels with me, showed the film, talked about it, referred to it in the lectures and workshops. It became a teaching film.

Learning is being able to see the relationship between things, and the more I talked about the film the more I learned from it. (I still think it's the best American screenplay written in the last 20 years.)

One overcast Saturday morning at the Palais des Beaux Arts I showed the film to some Dutch filmmakers, and then we sat around and discussed it in front of a large audience of participating writers from the European film community. I started talking about the midpoint, illustrating it with the scene in the parking lot, when I suddenly realized I was wrong. That wasn't the midpoint, because it tells us what we already know; the real midpoint is the scene right after it, when Gittes goes to see Yelburton, the new head of the Department of Water and Power. The secretary tells him that Yelburton will be tied up indefinitely. "I'll wait," Gittes says. He lights up a cigarette and plops down in the chair. "I take a long lunch. All day, sometimes."

He starts humming to himself, and we see the secretary become edgy. He gets up and prowls along the wall looking at the many photographs detailing the history of the department. There are several photographs of Hollis Mulwray and a man named Noah Cross standing together at various construction sites. Cross (John Huston) is the man Mulwray was arguing with outside the Pig 'n' Whistle early in the screenplay.

Cross. The name rings a bell. He takes out Evelyn Mulwray's envelope and looks again at the monogram ECM. He asks if Noah Cross worked for the water department. Flustered, the secretary says yes, then no. Noah Cross *owned* the water department, she says, along with Mulwray. They were partners. Mulwray felt the public should own the water; Cross didn't agree, and they had a falling out.

Something clicks for Gittes. Evelyn Mulwray is Noah Cross's daughter; that means she married her father's business partner. Whose side is Evelyn on—father's or dead husband's? Gittes suddenly realizes that Noah Cross could have a very strong motive for killing Hollis Mulwray.

This information is a vital link in the dramatic action of Act II; it is the first piece of information that points to the solution of the puzzle; it ultimately leads to Jake Gittes's proving that Noah Cross is the man responsible for the murders and the water scandal, and that he was guilty of incest. It is a link in the chain of dramatic action, an essential clue to Gittes's understanding of what's going on. *Chinatown*, remember, is a detective story; we learn what's going on at the same time Jake Gittes does.

"You may *think* you know what's going on," Cross tells Gittes early on, "but you don't." He still doesn't know but he is now on the way to finding out. Midpoint.

The connection between Evelyn Mulwray, Noah Cross, and Hollis Mulwray links the action of the first half of Act II with the second half of Act II. In the first half Gittes finds out *what's going on;* in the second half, he finds out *who's behind it.*

When I drew it on the *paradigm* it looked like this:

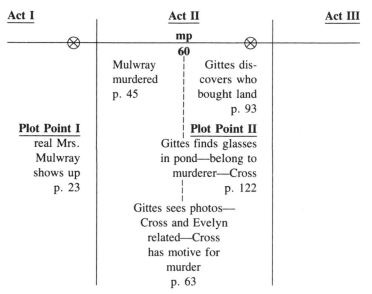

Act I	Act II	Act III

Once I saw that connection, the entire second act fell into place. When I looked at it, everything tied together, like the intricate weave of a sixteenth century Belgian tapestry. That information, that connection, that link in the chain of dramatic action, moves the story forward, step by step, scene by scene, plot point by plot point.

When you're writing Act II, you always have to know where you're going; you've got to have an end point, a goal, a destination. You must plan your character's course of action. What happens to your main character from Plot Point I to Plot Point II?

Knowing the midpoint is a tool; with it you have a way of focusing your story line into a specific line of action. You have a direction, a line of development. You can work with a 30-page unit of dramatic action, confident and secure that you know your story; you know where you're going and what you're doing.

What's the midpoint of your story? What is the incident, episode, event, line of dialogue, or decision that links the first half of Act II with the second half of Act II? Define it. Trace the action of your character to it and from it. Run it through your mind a few times. Check it out. Does it work?

Sometimes you may *arbitrarily* designate an incident as the midpoint only to find out during the actual writing that something else is the midpoint. If that happens, be prepared to change it.

One student was writing a screenplay about an actress up for a major part who becomes involved with an alcoholic; she learns she must let him go to get the part she wants. Originally, the author structured the story around the relationship with the alcoholic. But this took away from the action of the main character. The relationship, an old destructive pattern of behavior, represented the old way of life, the part represented a new beginning, a new way of life. The midpoint was the scene in which the actress first suspects that the man she's fallen in love with is an alcoholic.

But that didn't work. When my student completed her second act, she realized she had to change the midpoint because the story was about the actress getting the part; the midpoint now became the scene where she goes back for an audition. Changing the midpoint changed everything. It clarified the story line and made all the difference in the world

When you're writing, you have to go with what's working "right now." If you're ever caught in a creative dilemma and you don't know what to do, or which element is "right," always go with the present moment. Trust the screenwriting process. It's larger than you are.

Do what *feels right*. Don't worry about what you decided a long time back.

Things happen. People change. Things change.

The only question that's relevant is, does it work? If it does, use it; if it doesn't, don't. When you're writing and a new thought occurs, one you hadn't planned on or thought about, write it down; try it out.

When in doubt, write.

It's easier to cut than it is to add. If you want, write a 175-page words-on-paper draft. The worst that can happen is that you make a mistake. You'll have to go back and rewrite some pages. So what? In my workshops, we make an agreement that the workshop is going to be an educational opportunity; that means the willingness to make mistakes. Try things that may not work. It's the only way to grow and evolve, to sharpen your skills.

The midpoint is a pit stop, a destination, a beacon that guides you and keeps you on course during the execution of your story line.

E.T.—The Extra-Terrestrial, written by Melissa Mathison and directed by Steven Spielberg, is a case in point. Look at the story line. E.T. is left behind when his spaceship leaves planet Earth. Hunted as an alien, he wanders into the suburbs and is found and cared for by Elliott, a small boy, played by Henry Thomas. That's Plot Point I. It occurs on page 23.

During the first half of Act II, E.T. and Elliott become friends. Elliott introduces his visitor, "the goblin," to his brother and sister. Soon Elliott and E.T. are connected by feelings; Elliott feels what E.T. feels. And E.T. is homesick; he wants to go home. He wants to *phone* home. "E.T. phone home," he says to Elliott, and points out the window.

"And they'll all come?" the boys asks.

E.T. nods.

That's the midpoint. It happens on page 61.

The boys go into the garage and gather up whatever's around and take it to E.T.: a saw blade, a few toys, a soldering iron, a coffee can. And we're already being prepared for what's to come. Elliott's older brother says, "E.T. might be getting kinda sick." It sets up the entire second half of Act II.

E.T. takes the elements and spins them into a primitive communications system. At Halloween, wearing a goblin costume, E.T. escapes into the forest with the children.

E.T. sets up the communicator system and sends its signals deep into space. Elliott and E.T. spend the night in the forest. E.T. is not only homesick; he becomes physically sick. Then sicker. In a desperate plea for help, Elliott shows E.T. to his mother in the shower. But it's too late. E.T. is dying. "Please. Home," he says. That's Plot Point II. Page 86.

The adults take over. They try to save him, but it's no use. E.T. "dies."

Then miraculously comes back to life.

On the *paradigm*, it looks like this:

Act I	**Act II**		**Act III**
	m p		
⊗		⊗	
Plot Point I	"getting	"helping E.T.	
Elliott hides	acquainted"	phone home"	
E.T. in closet			
p. 23	E.T. wants to		
	phone home		
	p. 61		
		Plot Point II	
		E.T. dying	
		p. 86	

E.T.'s dramatic need to phone home leads to getting homesick, which leads to physical sickness, death, and his miraculous rebirth. The midpoint ties it all together.

The first time I read the script I noticed that the structure of the subplot—the pursuers tracking, then finding, E.T. —parallels the main action. After Plot Point I, on page 24, the pursuers hone in on the suburban area where E.T. is hiding. On page 64, right after the midpoint, they discover the exact house where E.T. is being hidden. On page 87 they move in and take over the house. I wondered if I was wrong and questioned my structural interpretation of the script. So I drew it out on the *paradigm*.

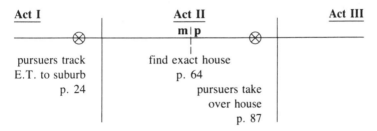

| **Act I** | | **Act II** | | **Act III** |

pursuers track E.T. to suburb p. 24

find exact house p. 64

pursuers take over house p. 87

I wondered if that was the "true" structure. But when I thought about it, I realized structure is a function of story, like an ice cube and water, or a fire and its heat. I asked myself one question: What is this story about? It is about the relationship between the boy and E.T.; it's not a story about the "adults" finding E.T. What your story is about dictates the structural elements of your dramatic action.

The midpoint is a link in the chain of dramatic action; it connects the first half of Act II with the second half. In *E.T.* it is a simple scene between Elliott and E.T. In *Chinatown*, it is a quiet scene in an office; photographs on the wall make an important story connection. In *Absence of Malice*, it is a dinner in a bar.

Written by Kurt Luedtke and superbly directed by Sydney Pollack, *Absence of Malice* is a very underrated film. Like Pollack's *Three Days of the Condor*, it moves like lightning; it is lean, clean, tight, and fast, and it makes the viewer and reader work to follow the story line. It is American filmmaking at its best.

An investigative reporter, Megan (Sally Field), is writing a story about a man (Paul Newman) under investigation for the murder of an underworld figure. The script opens with a special investigating strike force trying to find the person or persons responsible for the murder of Joey Diaz, an underworld racketeer. The strike force, led by Elliot Rosen (Bob Balaban) is looking at "home movies" of a funeral taken by the FBI many years before. We learn that the man they want to question is Michael Gallagher, the son of a former racketeer and rum-runner. This scene is an example of good screenwriting: it *visually* gives the audience necessary information about character, premise, and situation.

We meet Megan as she is sniffing around for a story. She knows something's going on with the strike force, but doesn't know what.

Elliot Rosen deliberately leaves Michael Gallagher's file for Megan to "find." Based on the information in the file, she thinks she has a story, a good story; a special investigation of Michael Gallagher which will possibly lead to the killer of Joey Diaz. The story she writes may not be true, but the paper prints it. "We have no knowledge the story is false, therefore we are absent of malice. We have been both reasonable and prudent, therefore we are not negligent. We may say what we like about Mr. Gallagher and he is powerless to do us harm. Democracy is served."

The paper is covered.

But not Michael Gallagher.

When Gallagher reads the story, he wants to find out who wrote it and the source. He goes to see Megan at the paper. "I'm Michael Gallagher," he says. "I want to know where this story comes from."

She spills her coffee. That's Plot Point I. It happens on page 31 (the screenplay is 134 pages long). This screenplay is one in which the main character doesn't appear until the end of Act I. Before you get too excited about that, though, notice that Michael Gallagher has been talked about and referred to from page 1. If you write a script like this, you still have to introduce your main character in the first ten pages. *Absence of Malice* is about Michael Gallagher; he is the main character. Megan, while a major character (and probably a larger part), is not the main character.

The first half of Act II deals with the reaction to the story. The police question Gallagher, the D.A. wonders if there is any truth to it, and Gallagher's uncle (Luther Adler), an old-time underworld figure, also wants to know if it's true. Everyone seems to behave as if the story were true. Megan, hungry for a followup, brazenly calls Gallagher and invites him to lunch, complete with microphone, tape recorder, and blundering photographer.

Gallagher surprises her by taking her to lunch aboard his yacht. Offshore, he begins to question her about the source of her newspaper story. He finds the tape recorder she has hidden, and to make things worse, a police helicopter swoops down on them and takes pictures. Gallagher is disappointed; he thought she might help him and now he knows differently; she wants her story, no matter the price he has to pay.

"Somebody wants something," he tells her. "I gotta

know who and what. I gotta know where that story came from.''

"I can't tell you that," she replies.

Gallagher is on his own.

The bank refuses to give him a loan, something they've done every year for years, and the union puts a picket line in front of the warehouse and shuts him down. He's got to find out who's behind that story. The only thing he can do is find Megan and possibly convince her to reveal her sources. It's a long shot, but it's either that or nothing.

He goes to the bar where she hangs out and buys her dinner. He says, "I need you to know me. . . . Fast." That's the midpoint; it happens on page 67.

That scene shifts the context from trying to find out "who's out to get him" to creating a "personal relationship with Megan"; it is a link in the chain of dramatic action. It connects the first half of Act II with the second half of Act II. When the story shifts into the personal relationship between Gallagher and Megan, it leads to his finding out "who's responsible." In 30 pages they learn a lot about each other, even get to like each other.

When Megan receives a call from Gallagher's friend Teresa (Melinda Dillon), Megan says that whatever she says might be in the paper. Teresa desperately tries to convince her that Michael is innocent of everything; he was with Teresa in Atlanta when Diaz was killed. She had an abortion, she confesses. "In the Church it's murder," she says. "I killed my child."

Megan thinks that's being a little *too* dramatic for this day and age, and doesn't take it seriously. She writes the story. The next morning, Teresa reads it; she's shocked, mortified, humiliated; unable to face family or friends, she commits suicide.

Megan is stunned, Gallagher broken. When she comes to see him and apologize, he lashes out at her. She breaks down and tells him that Elliot Rosen is the man in charge of the investigation. "He runs the strike force. He's the one who leaked the story about you."

That's the man he's been searching for. It is Plot Point II and occurs on page 89.

Act I		Act II		Act III
		m│p		
	⊗	**6│0**	⊗	
	reaction to story	│ relationship │ with Megan		
Plot Point I		│ **Plot Point II**		
Gallagher meets Megan p. 31		│ Gallagher │ learns Rosen │ is "source" │ p. 89		
		buys Megan dinner p. 63		

The midpoint shifts the action from the effect of the investigation to the personal relationship with Megan. Ultimately, it leads Gallagher to the information he needs to obtain. That's what the midpoint does: It is a link in the chain of dramatic action. When you establish it, it structurally connects the first half of Act II with the second half of Act II. It establishes a clear sense of direction in the second act, allowing you to focus on the specifics of your story. It is a beacon, a destination, a reference point, an end point, a guide through the complexities of Act II.

The script was restructured in the editing room; the paradigm of the film is:

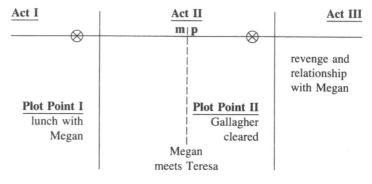

Act I | Act II | Act III
m | p
revenge and
relationship
with Megan

Plot Point I
lunch with
Megan

Plot Point II
Gallagher
cleared

Megan
meets Teresa

The Exercise

Look at the paradigm on the following page. Read the story line. Structure it into a dramatic entity. Determine the ending. Then the opening. Then Plot Point I and Plot Point II.

Now you are ready to find the midpoint.

Reread the story line. Lay it out on the *paradigm*. If necessary, review Chapter 4, "Four Pages." Now that you know your ending, your beginning, and Plot Point I and Plot Point II, determine your midpoint. What is the incident, episode, or event that connects the action of the first half of Act II with the second half of Act II?

Write it down.

When you've established the midpoint, you're ready to set up the dramatic context of Act II.

The Paradigm Structured

The Story: An American journalist, in Paris on a magazine assignment, meets a young French woman, a high-ranking and politically active member of the ministry of culture. They have an affair and fall in love. When he completes his assignment, he must return home, and as he boards the plane he swears he will return.

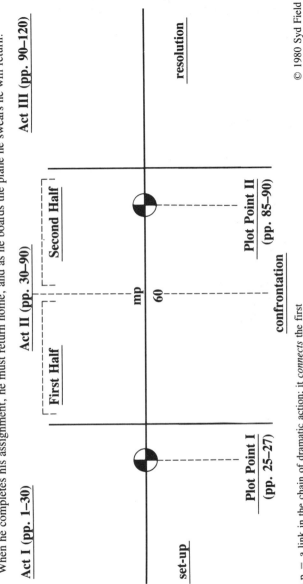

Act I (pp. 1–30)

set-up

Plot Point I
(pp. 25–27)

Act II (pp. 30–90)

First Half

Second Half

mp
60

confrontation

Plot Point II
(pp. 85–90)

Act III (pp. 90–120)

resolution

© 1980 Syd Field

m p = a link in the chain of dramatic action; it *connects* the first half of Act II with the second half of Act II.

13

First Half, Second Half

Wherein we define dramatic context and introduce the pinch:

Look at the *paradigm*:

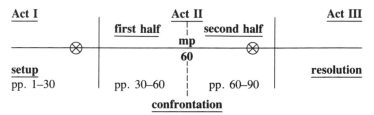

Act II is a unit of dramatic action that is 60 pages long and held together with the dramatic context known as *confrontation*. It starts at Plot Point I and continues to Plot Point II.

It is a unit of dramatic action that is broken down into two basic units that are 30 pages each, the first half of Act II and the second half of Act II, connected by the midpoint. Therefore, we have start points and end points in Act II.

It is a map, a guide; it gives us direction.

At this point in our screenwriting process, we start

working in units of action, the first half and second half. The first half of Act II starts at Plot Point I and goes to the midpoint; the second half of Act II goes from midpoint to Plot Point II.

Two 30-page units of dramatic action.

What happens in the first half of Act II? What does your main character do? Where does he or she go? What are the obstacles to his or her dramatic need? What happens from Plot Point I to the midpoint?

What *holds* it all together? That's the first thing you have to know. Once we determine the dramatic *context* of the first half, then we can provide the *content*, the individual scenes needed to make it work.

Context, remember, is the space *inside* the empty coffee cup; it *holds* the coffee in place. *Context* is the space that holds *content* in place.

What is the dramatic *context* of the first half of Act II?

What idea or principle holds the action in place? Can you describe it in a few words? Is it a relationship? A journey? The start of a vacation? Suddenly losing a job, or getting one? The beginning of a marriage?

Define it. Articulate it. Draw it on the *paradigm*.

In *Body Heat* Plot Point I is reached when Racine and Matty have sex for the first time. The first half of Act II deals with their relationship based exclusively on sex. *Body Heat*, after all, is a story of passion, lust, murder, and betrayal; it's hot and steamy and sexy. If we wanted to tell somebody what the first half of Act II was about in a few words, we could describe it as a sexual relationship in which the sexual partners "bonded" together as accomplices in murder.

It looks like this:

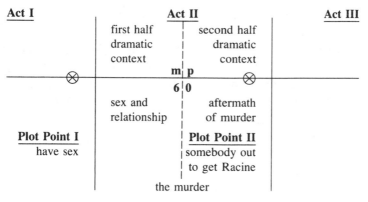

For most of the first half of Act II, Racine and Matty are having sex. Sure, we see him running, see a few shots of him alone, probably thinking about Matty, a scene in his office, but for the most part they are having sex. Then, on page 45, Matty says how nice it would be if her husband were dead. This little scene "pinches" the action together and keeps it on track.

From that point on, the dramatic context is no longer sex alone; the action now revolves around sex *and* talk about murder. Racine and Matty talk more and more about murdering her husband—under the guise of love, commitment, and relationship, of course.

That's what happens in the first half of Act II: that is the dramatic context—the idea, expressed in a few words, that "holds" the action in place.

In the second half, the context could be described as the "aftermath of murder." The entire 30-page unit of action deals with the details: removal of the body, setting the arson device to burn the Breakers Hotel, setting up an alibi, all frantic whisperings and rendezvous before the discovery of the body that leads to Plot Point II, the scene where Lowenstein tells Racine that somebody is setting him up.

Love and death, connected by the midpoint, the murder.

Once you determine your dramatic context for each half, you can design a line of action that executes your story line in the most dramatic fashion. That's what dramatic context does: It "holds" the action, the content, in place.

In *Absence of Malice*, the script Plot Point I occurs when Gallagher comes to see Megan at the paper after the story has been printed. The midpoint occurs when he buys her dinner, which leads to their beginning a relationship.

The first half of Act II deals with the reaction to the story: Newman is investigated, questioned, lied to, and shut down. He has nowhere to go and no one to turn to except the reporter who wrote the story, Megan. That's his only chance and he goes for it.

The second half deals with their relationship. They spend time together and make love. Teresa calls Megan and tells her that Gallagher is innocent because he was in Atlanta with her; Megan meets with Teresa, the story is printed, and Teresa commits suicide. Megan comes to Gallagher and Plot Point II occurs: She tells him the source of the story is Elliot Rosen. Act II deals with the *reaction to the story* in the first half, and the *relationship with Megan* in the second half. The dramatic context *holds* the action in place; 60 pages of action reduced to a few words.

That's the power of dramatic context; when you establish it, you have something to hang on to—a line of dramatic action going from Plot Point I to the midpoint, and from midpoint to Plot Point II.

Defining the dramatic context puts you in a position of choice—it gives you a basis for designing the action that is needed to tell your story. That's the function and the importance of the dramatic context. It *holds* everything together; it *is* structure.

Think about your story line. What happens in the first half of Act II? The second half? Think about it. Define it.

Once you define the context you can determine the time frame.

Aristotle considered *time, place,* and *action* to be the three unities that hold dramatic tragedy in place. In his *Poetics* he expressed the view that the time of action must correspond to the length of the play. A play of two hours could cover only two hours in the hero's life; the time of the play was the time of the action. Unlike the writer of an epic, who could represent years of action on a many-sided canvas of mythological proportions, a playwright was limited to a single action. We don't see Oedipus killing his father: we hear somebody tell about it.

That was the way it was until the sixteenth century, when Shakespeare and his contemporaries bridged the unity of time by portraying years in a character's life, while "this poor player struts and frets his hours upon the stage and then is heard no more." By dramatizing a scene here, a scene there, time was bridged, condensed, and held together by the vast spectacle of action.

Shakespeare's method was cinematic. What Homer did in his epics, and Shakespeare did in his plays, is basically what George Lucas and Steven Spielberg are doing today in their stories of myth and ritual and imagination. An epic like *Star Wars* cuts through space, age, and time.

If you're writing a screenplay that covers a period of years, what incidents do you show? What don't you show? What makes "this" incident more important than "that" incident? Stories covering years are difficult to write, and beginning screenwriters usually "scatter" the incidents like buckshot, hoping that luck, good fortune, and the muses will be with them. They usually are not.

Planning, preparation, and persistence are the keys to writing a successful screenplay. Figure out the time frame of your story. How long a period of time does it cover? *The Best Years of Our Lives? The Year of Living Dangerously? 48 Hrs.?*

Think about it.

If your action takes place over a three-day, or three-week, or three-month period, you can focus the action into a sharp visual presentation. The novel *Six Days of the Condor* by James Grady was changed to *Three Days of the Condor* in order to make it a tighter, leaner visual presentation to generate greater tension and drama.

You may decide that Act II takes place within a two-month period. The first half may be two weeks, the second half six weeks. The passing of time can be marked in several ways: by seasonal changes of clothing from summer to fall, winter, or spring; by dialogue references to specific days like Memorial Day, Labor Day, Christmas, or Halloween, or by the use of an event like an election, a birth, a wedding, or a funeral.

What is the time frame of Act II? (Don't worry about Act I, we'll return to that in Chapter 16, "The Rewrite.") Think about the first half of Act II: What is the time frame for your action? Decide how long or short it is. Find a workable time frame within which to operate. Trust your story; it will tell you what the time period is. Don't get too hung up with it. Don't make it *too* significant or important.

The time frame keeps your story in motion. It supports the context. No one needs to know what the context or time frame is except you.

When you begin to outline the action for the first half of

Act II, you have the dramatic context and the time frame to hold it together. You have direction, a line of development that will determine the action leading to the midpoint and from there to Plot Point II.

The importance of context and time frame is that it gives you greater structural support and enhances the dramatic tension by determining the obstacles your main character needs to overcome in order to achieve his or her dramatic need.

When you've done this for the first half of Act II, do it for the second half of Act II. The two units of action are separate and independent even though they are part of the larger whole of Act II.

That bring us to "the pinch."

When I was in Brussels doing the screenwriting workshop, I worked with three European screenwriters in front of a large audience. The writers actually wrote their scripts during the workshop. They would discuss their story and the pages coming up, the audience would raise questions about it, and they would then go home and write. The next week they would come in with 10 or 20 pages and we would read them together. Questions were asked and dramatic choices explained: Why is this scene better "here," than "there"? Why use the main character here and not another character? Can we change this scene to another locale, even another act?

We began working on the material for Act II. We started by outlining the action from Plot Point I to the midpoint. In one particular session, I was explaining how the dramatic context "held" the story in place and at the same time "moved" it forward. And before I knew it, I heard myself saying "All you need is one key scene to hold the entire first half of Act II in place."

I'm not sure why I said it, or where it came from. It just came out. It "felt right" when I said it, and, of course, the French filmmakers in the audience jumped right in and asked me to explain it.

Look at the *paradigm*:

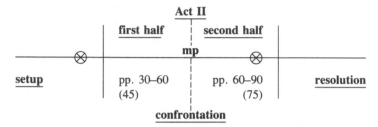

If you look at the first half of Act II, you'll see that all you need is one important scene or sequence, around page 45, to hold the entire 30-page unit of dramatic action in place. That's all you need to "hold" 15 pages together.

In *Chinatown*, Mulwray's murder on page 45 is enough to move the story forward to the midpoint, which then moves the story forward to the point where Gittes (Nicholson) discovers that land in the Northeast Valley has been sold to dead people or people in retirement homes. That moves the story forward so Gittes learns that Noah Cross is responsible for the murders as well as the water scandal.

That scene or sequence is just a little "pinch" to keep your story on track.

During the remainder of the Brussels workshop I made sure my screenwriters knew that one scene on page 45 and one on page 75 would keep their story on track. The writers loved working with these scenes.

Shortly after I returned home, I was invited by the Mill Valley Film Festival in Marin County to conduct a one day screenwriting workshop with Sam Shepard, who is one of

America's finest playwrights and an accomplished actor as well.

During the course of the day Shepard mentioned that when he had an idea for a play, he sat down and started writing; he said it took him about 15 pages to tell whether it was working or not. He explained that if he "found" something to use—a character, a back story, an incident—he knew he had a play and kept going. If he didn't, which happened more often than not, he knew the idea wasn't working and he shelved it; it wasn't strong enough, or dramatic enough, or whatever, to make a catching stage presentation. He's got a lot of those unfinished 15 pages lying around, he said.

And he is a prolific playwright.

Fifteen pages. You can do a lot in that.

In my workshops I confirmed that if you're looking at a 30-page unit of dramatic action, all you need is one major scene or sequence to tie it all together. You lead into that scene or sequence on page 45, then move to the mid-point on page 60, then to the scene on page 75, then to Plot Point II.

My students taught me about this. They told me it was the most important element in writing Act II. The term "pinch" cropped up over and over again, and I thought that was the appropriate label because this one scene or sequence "pinches" the story line together: It *ties it to-gether and keeps your story on track.*

So it became the "pinch." The main purpose is to *keep your story on track.*

Pinch I occurs around page 43 of the first half, Pinch II around page 75. A pinch can be a scene, a sequence, a plot point. In *Chinatown*, Mulwray's murder is Pinch I; it is a sequence as well as a plot point.

In *Body Heat*, Pinch I occurs on page 45 when Matty Walker tells Racine she wishes her husband were dead; and so begins the tale of lust, intrigue, and murder. Pinch II occurs on page 75 when her husband's glasses are found missing, someone wants to turn them in, and the police intensify their investigation, which leads to Plot Point II.

In *Absence of Malice*, Pinch I occurs when Megan and Gallagher are having lunch on board his yacht and he discovers the microphone and recorder she's hidden and wants to know "who the hell I'm talking to." It happens on page 47. Pinch II occurs on page 75, when Megan learns that Gallagher was with Teresa in Atlanta.

This is the way it looks:

```
                 first half    |    second half
                     |          m  p        |
                     |          |  |        |
  ⊗----------------+----------|--|-------+--⊗----------
                     |          |  |        |
                  Pinch I       |        Pinch II
                   (45)         |          (75)
```

In *Return of the Jedi*, Act I deals with the rescue of Han Solo from the clutches of Jabba the Hutt. The entire act deals with Solo's escape. Plot Point I occurs when they actually leave Totooine.

When they return home, Luke Skywalker seeks out the ancient and venerable Jedi, Yoda. In a touching and moving scene, the ancient philosopher tells Luke that before he can become a true Jedi knight, he must seek out and confront the "dark side of the Force"—his father, Darth Vader. And the old Jedi dies.

That's Pinch I; it keeps the story on track. It occurs on page 44, and here's what it looks like:

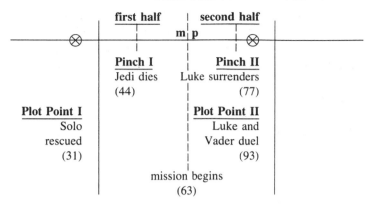

The midpoint occurs when the mission to destroy the "new" Death Star begins, and Pinch II occurs when Luke surrenders so he can confront his father. Plot Point II comes at the beginning of their duel, intercut with Solo and Princess Leia entering the passageway to lower the shield.

Usually there's a relationship between Pinch I and Pinch II, some kind of story connection. In *Return of the Jedi*, Pinch I has the dying Jedi telling Luke he must confront his father, and in Pinch II, Luke surrenders in order to confront his father.

In *WarGames,* superbly written by Lawrence Lasker and Walter Parkes, Plot Point I occurs when Matthew Broderick enters the computer program with "list games" and gains access to the WOPR computer. Pinch I occurs when he enters "Joshua" into the computer and plays Global Thermonuclear War; the midpoint is reached when he is arrested by the FBI, Pinch II occurs when he makes his escape, and Plot Point II is when he convinces Dr. Falken, creator of the computer, to return with him to NORAD. Everything ties together to "lock" the story on course. That's why Pinch I and Pinch II are the last things you'll determine before writing.

Your story always *unfolds,* so character, reader, and audience learn what's going on together. In *Chinatown* we learn what Jake Gittes learns.

The more I use Pinch I and Pinch II in my workshops, the more valuable I see they are. If you prepare for writing Act II by establishing the midpoint and then determining dramatic context and time frame, when you're ready to add Pinch I and Pinch II you will have an overview of Act II that keeps you moving through your story line with confidence and ease.

You must know where you are and where you're going. If you get lost when you're writing Act II, you'll spend days, perhaps weeks, of frustration trying to figure your way out of the maze of your creation.

When you're writing Act II, you have no objectivity at all, and if you doubt yourself in terms of material, you'll start censoring everything you write, and you won't be able to write anything. Don't let that happen. Keep writing no matter what you feel about it, good, bad, or indifferent. Judgments and evaluations of your work will rise with regular persistence. Just write your story, page by page, scene by scene, shot by shot.

Breaking Act II into first and second half, then establishing dramatic context and time frame, then Pinch I and Pinch II, will allow you to gain a structural overview that keeps your story on track. It will guide you through the obstacle course of Act II.

The Exercise

Let's do the following exercise as a "tune-up."

Look at the *paradigm* (on the next page): the story, about a young woman in an unhappy marriage enrolling in an art class and having an affair with her teacher, is at the top of the page.

The way it's broken down and structured is the same way we structure all our exercises: ending first, then beginning, then Plot Points I and II, then midpoint, then dramatic context for the first half, second half, time frame, and pinch.

In Act I we set up the story. We're going to set up and show the unhappy marriage of our main character in Act I. Plot Point I occurs when she enrolls in the art class.

Since she has an affair with her teacher, and becomes pregnant at Plot Point II, the midpoint should be when she sleeps with him for the first time. The dramatic context establishes the relationship with the teacher, so we focus on that aspect of the story in the first half of Act II. The second half deals with falling in love with the teacher.

Look at it on the *paradigm,* first half and second half.

Go over the action. What do you think Pinch I is?

It might be where the young woman and the teacher have an opportunity to get to know each other for the first time on a one-to-one basis. Maybe she wants an appraisal of her work and they go out for coffee after class; or her car won't start in the parking lot and he helps her get it started; or he gives her a ride home and they decide they like each other; or they meet at a party. Any such situation will work as Pinch I.

The Paradigm Structured

The Story: A young woman in an unhappy marriage, a painter, enrolls in an art class and has an affair with her teacher. She falls in love with him and then learns she is pregnant. Caught in the web of circumstance, she finally resolves to leave both husband and lover and have her child on her own.

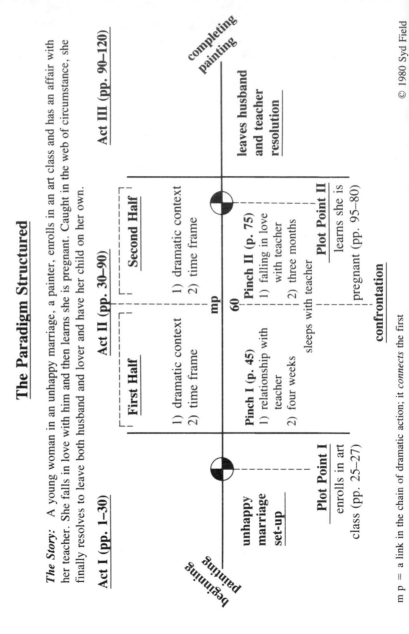

Act I (pp. 1–30)

Act II (pp. 30–90)

Act III (pp. 90–120)

beginning painting

completing painting

Plot Point I
enrolls in art class (pp. 25–27)

unhappy marriage set-up

First Half

1) dramatic context
2) time frame

Pinch I (p. 45)
1) relationship with teacher
2) four weeks

sleeps with teacher

mp

60

Second Half

1) dramatic context
2) time frame

Pinch II (p. 75)
1) falling in love with teacher
2) three months

Plot Point II
learns she is pregnant (pp. 95–80)

confrontation

leaves husband and teacher
resolution

© 1980 Syd Field

m p = a link in the chain of dramatic action; it *connects* the first

Our character is not about to jump right into bed with her teacher, no matter how unhappy she might be with her husband. She is cautious, and her actions will be appropriate to the circumstances. Otherwise, we don't have any sympathy for her, and your main character must always be sympathetic. Just look at how unsympathetic Richard Gere is in *Breathless*; we don't like his character at all, thus the dismal audience reaction at the box office.

Student and teacher spend time together and then, at the midpoint, make love. Page 60. That gives you 15 pages of script, or 15 minutes of screen time, to visually reveal their relationship.

During the second half of Act II the student falls in love with her teacher, leading to Plot Point II, where she learns she's pregnant. It could be a scene in a doctor's office, or the results of a pregnancy test. If they have an intense and passionate scene making love, it will be where she conceives.

What do you think Pinch II is? Think about it. Study the *paradigm*. Write down a few ideas.

going to the doctor's office
a fight with her husband
a fight with the teacher
leaving her husband
telling the teacher she loves him
learning the teacher has a wife
a weekend trip where they make love and she conceives

Any will work. You decide.

I know what I would do: Pinch II is where she misses her period. That incident sets up choices: abortion; telling her husband; leaving her husband; leaving both husband

and lover and having the baby on her own and starting life all over again as a single person, mother, and painter.

You don't have to use *my* ending. You may have a different one. The dramatic choices listed work. The right one is the one that works for you.

If it works, use it; if it doesn't, don't. That's the rule. Make some mistakes. Try it. When you are writing a screenplay you've got to be open and receptive to all those little "accidents" that mysteriously happen on the blank sheet of paper.

Don't get too hung up in what you *want* to happen; let it happen. Screenwriting is a process, it continually changes and endures.

That's the real joy of writing.

14

Writing Act II

Wherein we put words down on paper:

You're ready to start writing the second act.

Prepare your material. Draw your story line on the paradigm. Separate Act II into first and second half. Establish your midpoint.

Determine the dramatic context for the first half of Act II.

Establish the time frame.

Then Pinch I.

Now lay out the first half of Act II in fourteen 3 × 5 cards, the same as you did for Act I.

Start from Plot Point I and go to the midpoint. Lay the cards out, one by one. Free-associate; put no more than a few words on each card; "Michelle at work," "lunch with Randy," "at swimming practice," "interviewed by sports reporter," "at home," "argument with mother," "runs to Randy's house," and so on. Short, brief, simple, concise statements that help move your story forward to the midpoint. Focus on those scenes that "fill" the context for the first half.

Find the elements, or components of the action based on the dramatic context. If your context is a young woman in an unhappy marriage, an artist, dramatize and reveal the context through her relationship with her husband; with her painting; with her friends, and with herself; these four elements will fill an entire 30-page unit of action.

When you're finished, go over the cards several times. If you need to, change a few words here, a few words there, maybe even a scene or two. Make the story line clean and simple; don't clutter it up with too many details, with twists and turns of plot. Go from the general to specific.

Once you know the action of the first half you're ready to write.

Write the first ten pages.

At this point, following Plot Point I, you're starting to feel comfortable with the form. You'll be making some mistakes and changes.

Design your scenes. Reread Chapter 10 of *Screenplay,* "The Scene." If a new scene comes to mind, write it down. If you leave the story line as written on the 3 × 5 cards, don't worry about it. Just keep writing. The cards are the cards and the screenplay is the screenplay. If you start writing new scenes, go with it; you'll always come back to the 3 × 5 cards when you need to.

You can leave the action you wrote on the cards, and go off in an entirely new direction, and before you know it, you're writing a scene you had on your cards. I don't know *why* it happens or *how* it happens—all I know is that it *does* happen. It's the writing process; it's larger than we are.

The first 10 pages may be stilted and awkward. That's okay. You're shifting from one mode into another so give yourself time to adjust to the first pages of words on paper.

Be clean and tight; don't clog up the action with a lot of

description or dialogue, or new plot twists and surprises. The context is *confrontation*; your character is confronting obstacles that keep him or her from achieving his or her dramatic need.

Move into the second 10 pages. You're leading into Pinch I, so design these second 10 pages carefully. What scenes do you have to write before you get to the pinch?

Describe them. Define them. Write them. Follow your story line.

Write Pinch I.

If it's too long, with too many scenes, or pages, don't worry about it. If you are in doubt about whether to write a scene or not, write it. It's always easier to cut out scenes than it is to write new ones.

Remember your visual dynamics. Open up your story, visually, cinematically. Do your scenes go from INT. to INT. to INT. to INT. with no EXT. scenes at all? Think about your transition, those lines of description or dialogue that take you from one scene to the next. Can you show your character walking out of the building? Taking a cab? In crowded traffic? Walking into a building? Riding in an elevator? Arriving at the airport? The plane in flight? Landing at the airport? In the baggage area? Show it. Think visually. Open up your story. Go from INT. to EXT. to INT. to INT. to EXT. (as an example). Be aware of visual transitions.

Don't describe too much or explain too much, and don't end up with "thick" paragraphs. Leave wide margins, left and right, at top and bottom. You want a lot of space on the page. Be sparse and simple in your descriptions, using no more than 5 or 6 sentences for each one. Read a screenplay, a good screenplay; reread the excerpts in *Screenplay: Chinatown, Network, Silver Streak, The Run.*

Sometimes you may have to write a full scene—beginning, middle and end—before you discover you can cut it down to a portion of the beginning and a few lines of the end.

Forget about camera angles and technical information. Don't show the reader how much you know. Simply write in master scenes, INT. OFFICE — DAY, and go from there.

Move into the third 10 pages of the first half. You're getting ready to write your midpoint, so design your scenes with that in mind. Keep moving forward; forget about perfect pages. Hold all your changes for the rewrite. That is when you'll integrate all those changes you've made during the actual writing.

Your writing will feel comfortable now, and your characters will be talking to you, telling you what *they* want to do, where *they* want to go. Go with the process. Don't be too dogmatic about staying in control.

Follow the focus of your main character; have the character initiate things, cause things to happen; your main character is active, not passive. Action is character; what a person does is what he is, not what he says.

Write the midpoint. Make sure it is a "link in the chain of dramatic action," connecting the first half of Act II with the second half of Act II.

We're working with 30-page units now, so once you've written the first half of Act II, prepare the second half, then write it. Determine the dramatic context, then the time frame, then Pinch II.

Do the 3 × 5 cards, 14, the same as the first half. Indicate Pinch II, then go over and over the cards until the line of action flows smoothly.

Write the first 10 pages of the second half. Just tell your

story, don't worry about frills or gimmicks. Make sure you are clear on your dramatic context and time frame.

Again, work in 10-page units, moving the action forward through Pinch II to the plot point at the end of Act II. If you want to clean up your 10-page sections, do it. Then move on. Always move forward from beginning to end, beginning to end. Don't spend time rewriting now. You'll do that later.

Just keep writing, moving forward, page by page, scene by scene, from midpoint to Pinch II to Plot Point II. Writing, remember, is a day-by-day process, 3 pages a day, five days a week; or if you have a full time job, think about the 10 pages you're going to write, then in two sessions sit down and do them. You can do 10 pages a week easily.

As you're writing you'll become aware of judgments and decisions and evaluations that are going to pop up with regular persistence. Suddenly you'll know a line of dialogue doesn't ring true, that you're forcing it; you *know*, deep down inside yourself, that what you're writing is not working; you'll know that it's not very good.

You might think to yourself, if *these* pages are bad, what about the other pages I've written? You might go back and read some of the pages you've written. And you know they're terrible. Awful.

Fear and panic and insecurity grip your heart; your mind begins racing. What am I doing? This story doesn't work at all. You try to calm yourself, but it's impossible. What to do? Drink? Drugs? Depression? Sex? A buying spree? Vacation? Isolation? Loss of identity?

You need some help, you might reason, an "assessment." You call a friend to read your pages. You might expect the worst, but deep down you know what you want to hear.

Your friend reads what you've written, and *confirms* your doubts and fears, saying, "I think your pages are fine, there's nothing wrong with them." Of course, they're lying, they're not telling you the truth, they're just trying to be nice, to save your feelings.

Or your friend will tell you your pages are not strong enough; they're "too wordy," or the focus should be on another character, and what you should do is this, and they give you an elaborate example of what they think your story is about. Of course, *they* don't know because *you* don't know.

At this point, you're over the edge in paranoia, and you don't know anything. You're "stuck inside a mobile, with those Memphis blues again," as Bob Dylan sings.

Many people just stop right there. They believe their own judgments, their own evaluations, their own opinions. They become their own victims. The truth is you can't see anything right now; you have no objectivity and no overview at all.

What you wrote may *not* be very good. Most of the first half is not going to be very good. Writing Act II will be about the same as writing Act I, except that the form is easier, and by now you've built up enough discipline so that you can sit down for a few hours each day and work on your script. But you're making more changes now than in Act I. And that sometimes creates a problem. It's easy to get lost or confused in the maze of your own creation.

This insecurity acts as a trigger, springing judgments and opinions into play. There's only one thing you must remember about your judgments and evaluations: *who* is making them?

You answer that one.

You can either let your judgments and evaluations get in

the way of your writing experience or not. It's up to you. You *do* have a choice; you *do* have a voice, a say in the matter. Use it.

If you find your mind racing, criticizing what you're writing, there is an exercise you can do to quiet your mind. Simply *give the critic a voice*.

When you're writing your pages, the "critic" part of you that's at the back of your head will be relentless and unmerciful. It will hound you, harass you, and hassle you. You're going to have to deal with it sometime—it might as well be now.

Give the critic a voice. Take a blank sheet of paper. Put it near your work pages. Now there are two sheets of paper in front of you—one for the script, the other for "the critic." Title it the Critic's Page.

Start writing. Soon you'll notice some familiar thoughts and judgments coming up. Write these negative thoughts and judgments (they're *never* positive, unfortunately) on the Critic's Page.

Continue writing your script. When another negative thought or judgment or doubt crops up, simply write it down. You might want to number them.

Give the critic a voice. When one page is filled, use another page. If you're like me, you're probably going to be writing more on the Critic's Page than on your script pages, but in a few days it will equal out; when you're through for the day, place the Critic's Pages in the drawer and forget about them.

Within a short time, maybe a week or two, you won't even need the Critic's Page. After all, your negative thoughts are *only* judgments, opinions, and evaluations. In the larger scheme of things, they don't mean too much.

Everybody has them. We either let them get in the way

of what we want to do, or we sidestep them. If we react too intensely, or too seriously, we can easily become our own victims.

And I speak from experience.

"Perfection," Jean Renoir used to tell me, "is an ideal. It exists only in the mind, not in reality."

That's something to think about.

Around page 45 or 50, around Pinch I, you may find your structure needs to be altered. If you need to restructure your story, do it. Structure is flexible. Scenes and passages of dialogue can be moved or repositioned.

Until a few years ago, buildings in Los Angeles and San Francisco could not be more than 12 stories high because of the earthquake hazard. Now high rise buildings are going up everywhere; they are designed to give, that is, to sway back and forth during a quake, bending with the shock of the earth moving. Nature is too strong to resist; bend with it.

Structure is like that; it can bend to the needs of your story. That's why the *paradigm* is not a formula; it is *form* that fits the needs of your story.

One of my students was writing a comedy about a young girl who in 1963 loses her virginity in a tacky, awful, first sexual encounter and becomes pregnant. In the end she journeys to Mexico for an abortion, and returns just as John Kennedy is assassinated. It is more than just a "losing virginity" story; it is the story about a young girl coming of age.

Originally, the structure was this: at Plot Point I she sees the boy she wants to sleep with; in Pinch I she is fitted for a diaphragm; at the midpoint she has sex with the boy, and Pinch II is her discovery that she's pregnant; at Plot Point II she leaves for Mexico to have the abortion. Act III deals with the abortion and her return home, a lot older and wiser.

When my student started writing and began to build the relationship between her main character and her two best friends, she realized she needed more time and pages to reveal their friendship. So she did it, and by the time she reached her supposed midpoint, her main character hadn't even been fitted for the diaphragm!

She became anxious and concerned, and I told her to simply change the structure and expand her story line. I told her we had to bend with the story and move the structural elements to fit the new story needs. So Plot Point I became a scene in which the girl makes the decision to lose her virginity that summer. Pinch I became a party where she sees the boy she wants to have sex with. He doesn't want anything to do with her. The new midpoint has her being fitted for her first diaphragm, Pinch II is her loss of virginity, and at Plot Point II she becomes pregnant. Mexico would be a very small sequence in Act III.

All she had to do was shift the structure to accommodate the needs of the story. Structure "holds" the story together, but it can bend and be shifted to include whatever new elements you need to put in.

When you're writing Act II, your story will be changing. You'll write one scene, then find you need to add another scene that will dramatize an aspect of your story you hadn't thought of when you were doing the cards. Go with it. Let it change. Right now, you are finding the focus of your story and it is shifting around because you can't "see" what you've written; you have no objectivity, no overview; you're just climbing the mountain.

The *paradigm* structure is a roadmap of your screenplay. You *can* get off the main highway and go exploring.

Writing *is* an adventure. If you do get lost or confused and don't know where you are or where you're going, go back to the *paradigm*; choose a plot point, a pinch, or the midpoint and start from there. It's only temporary. Just tell your story.

When you're *in* the paradigm you can't *see* the paradigm.

You'll learn how to adapt from your story. Learning, after all, is discovering the relationship between things. I learned that while I was preparing this chapter.

I take a lot of hot baths when I'm working, and I do a lot of work in the tub—preparing new material, planning the next scene or chapter, and so on. Dalton Trumbo worked in his bathtub a lot, as does Nick Meyer (*The Seven-Per-Cent Solution, Time After Time,* and *Star Trek II*).

My bathtub sits next to a large three-sided bay window; it has a large stationary pane in the middle and two smaller windows on either side.

One day while I was taking a bath, a large black bumble-bee found its way into the bathroom and couldn't find a way out. He circled the room, then gathered speed and flew directly into the large middle pane of glass. He tried again and again, and the same thing happened over and over again. I tried to stifle my panic as the rage and panic of the bee became louder and louder.

I watched the bee slamming into the window for what seemed an eternity, knowing that all he had to do to get free was stop, rest a moment, get his bearings, and take another look to see if there was another way out. The open window, fresh air, and escape were only three inches away.

Couldn't he see, I wondered, that what he was doing wasn't working? As this drama unfolded, I wondered whether I had ever done the same thing, pursued something—a job, a screenplay, a scene, a relationship—trying to make work what wasn't working, holding on to a part of my life and resisting a change that was as inevitable as night turning into day. I thought about it and recalled many episodes in my life when I had pursued something that wasn't working, that I knew would never work, with the same intensity as that bee slamming into the solid pane of glass.

Emotion welled up inside me. Yes, I *had* done that, I knew, and more than once. I still do it, and probably will do it again. It's a universal experience, one we all share, human as well as bee.

I watched that bee lunge into that glass again and again. I started getting angry. I wanted him out of my bathroom. I wasn't going to chase him or kill him, I just wanted him out. I thought to myself, Bee, just stop what you're doing. It's not working. Admit it, face it, confront it, deal with it. The open window, escape to freedom, is only inches away.

Angry, I focused on the bee. Like magic, the bee stopped, resting on the glass. Silence. I held my breath, afraid to move. Then the bee arched back, felt the stream of fresh air through the open window, and was gone.

I breathed a sigh of relief. A wave of emotion surged through me. I had shared a common experience with that bee, learned from him, and all the sadness and unhappiness and despair and pain of remembered moments filled me. Tears welled up in my eyes. It was a somber, profound moment.

"Trying to make something work that wasn't working" has often happened when I was writing a script. I'd get lost or confused about my story and then wander around searching to get back on track, not knowing where I was or where I was going. What I was doing wasn't working. I thought if I was persistent enough, and kept working and working and working, "hitting my head against the typewriter," I would eventually find a way out of my confusion.

It never worked.

One of my students was writing a contemporary romantic comedy about a single mother, a successful career woman, who has been in a relationship with a psychiatrist for four years. When the story opens, the therapist, a successful author and also a single parent, will not commit himself to marriage.

In the back story, the relationship has been through several upheavals. At Plot Point I the main character severs the relationship "for good" and joins a support group for people who have been in dead-end relationships. The first half of Act II deals with the sudden appearance of the ex-husband after an absence of five years. He won't leave her alone. She resists as much as she can, then finally, in defiance and humor, gives in.

She reestablishes the relationship with her ex-husband. What didn't work the first time doesn't work the second time, and she ends her involvement with her ex-husband. The midpoint occurs when she makes the resolve to "make it or break it" with the psychiatrist.

Everything in the script was working except for the first half of Act II. The appearance of the ex-husband never worked within the context of the story line, as funny or as cute as it might have been. The play was based on a true story, and the author was determined to make it work, come hell or high water. She wrote four totally different versions of the first half of Act II, and none of them worked. The context, the relationship with the ex-husband, never worked to begin with; either the main character was unsympathetic or the ex-husband was unlikable.

Finally, my student threw her pages down in despair and disgust, lost, confused, angry, panicked. So I told her the story of the bumblebee. The first half of Act II wasn't working, and she just better stop slamming against the windowpane.

Reluctantly, she agreed.

In the revised version, when the ex-husband shows up, she tells him to get lost; she becomes antimen. With her newfound independence she becomes even more attractive, and the humor comes out of her interaction with men. The midpoint stayed the same.

If you find your material is not working, just stop and rethink it. If it works, it works; if it doesn't, it doesn't. The things you try that don't work will show you what does work. You have to make these creative mistakes in order to keep the focus on your story line.

The moral of the story is simple: if you do get lost, or confused, if you're trying to make something work that doesn't work, just stop and take a look around; see if you're slamming against a windowpane.

Rethink it. You're working in 10-page segments of a 30-page unit of dramatic action. You can always find out where you are; just go back and look at your story on the *paradigm,* possibly shift your structural components, or change the dramatic context. Ask your characters what you should do; they'll tell you what you need to know.

By the same token give yourself a pat on the back if something works the way you thought it would.

Be willing to change some of your elements to make your story line work.

Confusion is the first step toward clarity.

The Exercise

It's time to sit down and "do it."

You've prepared your material well.

Start from Plot Point I and go to the midpoint. Work in 10-page units, keeping Pinch I clearly in mind. Focus on conflict. Remember, if you know your character's dramatic need, you will be able to create obstacles to that need so your story becomes your character overcoming all obstacles to achieve his or her dramatic need. Create your character's point of view in a scene, then create the opposite point of view. If your character is an actress reading for a major part, make the director think she's not right for it. She's the wrong type, the wrong size, whatever, and your scene will have her convincing him that she *is* right for the part.

That's how you create conflict on the page and avoid it in your writing experience.

The hardest thing about writing is knowing what to write.

15

Act III:
The Resolution

Wherein we resolve the story:

Act III is a 30-page unit of dramatic action that starts at Plot Point II and extends through to the end of your screenplay. It is held together by the dramatic context known as resolution.

Resolution means "to find a solution; to explain or make clear; to break up into separate elements or parts." It is not the end of your story, it is the solution of your screenplay.

What happens to your main character? Does he live or die? Succeed or fail? Marry or divorce? Blow up the new Death Star or not? Recover his stolen merchandise or not? Regain the heavyweight championship of the world? Audition before the board of admissions? What *is* the resolution of your story?

In *Return of the Jedi* there are two major story forces unresolved at Plot Point II: one, the Rebel Alliance has to break the "protective shield" surrounding the new Death Star so the attack led by Billy Dee Williams can destroy the weapon. To achieve that, Han Solo and Princess Leia are on a mission to knock out the power source of the shield.

That's one story point. The other is to resolve the classic confrontation between good and evil, in this case, Luke Skywalker and Darth Vader, father and son. Will Luke succumb? Does he have the strength and courage to overcome Darth Vader? Can he survive the last "trial by fire" ritual and become the last Jedi knight?

"Resolution" means to "break up into separate elements" and "explain or make clear." These two story points have been set up from the beginning of Act II and now they have to be resolved. Luke does kill his father, but not before he repents and takes off his mask. The emperor *is* killed, and the "Good Side of the Force" is victorious.

The story is resolved in Act III. The end of the film is the victory celebration when Luke confides to Princess Leia that they are brother and sister. The Greeks and Romans used to end their plays this way.

This may seem like a trite resolution to some, but if you look at the classic American genre films of the last few decades—from *The Wild Bunch* (where everybody dies), to *Hud* (where the "hero" is still the same son of a bitch at the end as he was at the beginning), to *The French Connection* and *Apocalypse Now* and *Coming Home*—you will see that they reflect changing American attitudes toward apathy, protest, and war during the decades of the fifties, sixties, and seventies.

In the eighties another force is at work: survival. If humanity is to survive, if the earth is to survive, we must turn our energies into helping each other and saving the earth. If we don't, humanity will be the dinosaur of the modern epoch. Even if we continue to pollute the environment, even if we unleash our nuclear weapons and destroy ourselves, the earth will survive. It will simply retreat into another ice age, or a new volcano age, and after a couple of hundred thousand years or so a new species will emerge and the life cycle of the earth will repeat itself.

The earth *is* life. We are *one* species despite our differences in culture, color, and heritage. We all have the same needs and wants but express them differently.

Native Americans (formerly called American Indians) believe that the earth is a living being, and *all* life forms are part of that. Everything is related, and when we kill anyone or anything, either by pollution or weapons, we are our own victims.

We can stop it. If we are to survive as a species, we must learn to live with each other, help each other, and thus save each other. This is the attitude emerging during the eighties, and Hollywood reflects it. Happy uplifting, positive endings are seen in *Return of the Jedi, Absence of Malice, WarGames, Flashdance,* and *E.T.*

Death, violence, and nuclear annihilation are out. If you think an up, happy, or positive ending is simplistic or banal, take a look at the fairy tales, myths, epics, and adventures that have formed the basis of literature since the beginning of the written word. Greek tragedies *ennoble* the characters and humankind. The classic tragedies "enrich" the human condition and it's worthwhile to remember this. In the eternal conflict between good and evil, does evil *ever* win?

Never.

That's just the way it is. In the long run, good always triumphs over evil.

Be aware of it.

If you are wondering whether to make your ending "up" or "down," you have a choice; think "positive" and "feeling good." Think of *Flashdance* and *WarGames*. That's where the market is. Twenty years from now, it may be different.

But that's then, and this is now.

What *is* the resolution of your story? When you establish that, you can decide on the specific ending. You've always known your ending, now you can execute it. But first, does your ending still work? Is it still effective? Do you have to change the ending because of the changes you've made during the first two acts? Have you thought of another ending, a new one, more dramatic, more visual than the first one?

Don't think too much about it, just do it. If you try to figure out the "correct," the "right" ending, you'll never do it. Choose an ending that works, that fits your story. As you write it, you'll find out whether it's effective or not.

Trust the process. It's larger than you are; like "the Force," it will be with you if go with it; don't fight it and don't get in the way by forcing something to work that doesn't work.

Many people ask if there's a pinch or plot point in Act III. Sometimes there is, it depends on the needs of your story. A key scene may be needed to "connect" the resolution with the rest of your story line.

Resolve character and story. Does your character change during your screenplay? If so, pay it off in Act III. Show it visually, dramatically, to resolve your story. In *Annie Hall* a character is resolved, in *Absence of Malice,* a story.

In *Annie Hall*, Alvy Singer does not change, he is the same at the end of the screenplay as he was at the beginning. Cynical, filled with self-pity and doubt, he wants Annie Hall to fit his pictures or expectations of what *he thinks* a relationship should be. Remember the lobster scene in the kitchen? Annie and Alvy are cooking lobsters and both are afraid to stick them into the boiling water. It's a beautiful scene, as memorable as a Marx Brothers scene from *A Night at the Opera* or *Duck Soup*. In Act III, after Annie has left Alvy for Tony Lacey (Paul Simon), he tries to recreate the lobster scene with a different woman. Same setting, same situation, same action, only now the result is different; it is forced, contrived, unfunny.

Alvy Singer is a character who resists personal change throughout the script, and it is a key element in the success of the film. In the opening monologue, Alvy says, "I wouldn't want to belong to any club that would accept me as a member. That's the key joke of my adult life in terms of my relationships with women." It is prophetic, because it is paid off at the end. Annie changes, he doesn't.

The script ends with a monologue: "She had moved back to New York. She was living in SoHo with some guy. And when I met her she was, of all things, dragging him in to see *The Sorrow and the Pity*. Which I counted as a personal triumph . . . and I-I thought of an old joke, you know, this-this-this guy goes to a psychiatrist and says, 'Doc, uh, my brother's crazy. He thinks he's a chicken.' And, uh, the doctor says, 'Well, why don't you turn him in?' And the guy says, 'I would, but I need the eggs.' Well, I guess that's pretty much how I feel about relationships. You know, they're totally irrational and crazy and absurd and . . . but, uh, I guess we keep goin' through it because, uh, most of us need the eggs."

His character is consistent; at the end, he's alone, as cynical and resistant and set in his ways as he always was. His unwillingness to change, expand, and grow leads him to this point. Sad, yet moving; a perceptive and universal comment about the "human condition."

Absence of Malice resolves a story. At the end of Act II, Gallagher knows Elliot Rosen of the strike force is the man who launched the investigation against him. When Act III begins, two story components need to be resolved. He must clear himself of any wrong doing and resolve his relationship with Megan.

Once Gallagher knows who's responsible, he goes after them and gets his revenge. The first thing he does is buy a telephone answering machine, then makes a withdrawal at the bank (payable to the "Citizens for a Better Miami"), then telephones Quinn, the D.A., and arranges a meeting. His phone, needless to say, is being tapped illegally by Rosen. On the park bench, the site of their meeting, Gallagher tells the D.A. he will find out all he can about the murder of the underworld racketeer and will report his findings only if there is a public statement clearing him. Quinn says he'll see what he can do.

Gallagher comes to Megan's apartment to apologize, and they make peace and end up spending the night together. He leaves at dawn.

Quinn makes a public statement clearing Gallagher. Which means that somebody screwed up when the investigation was made public in the newspaper. Megan is being set up by Rosen to take the fall. "I don't get it," Megan's source says. "Quinn just blew the whistle on both of us," Megan says. "*You* went after the wrong guy. *I* wrote it."

Rosen, in revenge for the statement clearing Gallagher, sets out to indict both Quinn and Gallagher.

A story is released, written by Megan, that the D.A. is being bribed by Gallagher, and then all hell breaks loose. Nobody knows what's going on, and everybody is embarrassed. Gallagher's revenge is complete. Even his under-world uncle (Luther Adler) is pleased. "His father's son," he proclaims proudly.

And this brings us to the key confrontation scene in Act III. A special inquiry has been ordered by Wells, the assistant attorney general in charge of the organized crime division of the Department of Justice. He tells everybody involved that he wants to find out "what in the good Christ is goin' on around here." He wants Megan to tell him who her source was for the story of the D.A. being involved. "You know and I know that we can't tell you what to print and what not to," he says to Megan and her attorney. "We hope that you people in the press will act responsibly and when you don't, there ain't a helluva lot anybody can do about it. But we can't have people wanderin' around leakin' stuff for their own reasons. It's not legal . . . and worse'n that . . . it's not *right*." He looks directly at Megan and wants to know "where that story came from."

"The person who told me about the investigation of Mr. Quinn," she replies. "They weren't leaking it. They never intended it to be in the paper. I did that on my own. I'd tell you who it was in a minute. But if I do, you'll have to do something about it. And somebody else will be hurt. (A sad smile.) So it's really very simple, isn't it? It always was. I can hurt someone. (Pause.) Or I can . . . not hurt someone. No system . . . no laws . . . no rules. Just me. So . . . I can't tell you. If I have to go to jail, I'll just have to go to jail."

It is a moving and sincere statement of responsibility and dedication, a far cry from the opening scene where she simply writes her story without thinking about the consequences. For every action, there's an equal and opposite reaction.

Quinn is forced to resign as D.A. and Elliot Rosen is fired. At the end, Michael Gallagher is on his boat ready to cast off when Megan appears. They resolve their relationship. "What do we do now, Michael?" she asks. He looks at her steadily, smiles, and says simply, "Why don't you get me a beer." Fade out. The end.

Act III of *Absence of Malice* is an excellent example of a dramatic showdown and is everything a final confrontation scene should be; it is good drama *and* it resolves (reveals the solution of) the story. The whole thing is tied together by isolating the two dramatic elements needed to resolve the story.

When you prepare Act III, the first thing you must do is define the story elements. Isolate them. Try to find a key scene that will hold everything. Then lay out Act III on fourteen 3 × 5 cards.

Go over the cards until you feel comfortable with the story's progression. Then start writing. You'll find you'll be on automatic, comfortable with the writing and discipline and story line. You still won't know whether it's working or not, because you can't *see* anything, but it feels good. At this stage, it will be working in spite of your doubts or insecurities. Just keep writing. Trust the process. Lay it down, scene by scene, page by page.

All you have to do to complete Act III is put in time in front of the writing pad, typewriter, or computer screen.

You may even start thinking about your next screenplay.

Things will be going smoothly and easily until the last few pages of the script. Then you might feel strange, find yourself "blank," not knowing what to write and without any real desire to complete the screenplay. You'll look for, and find, every excuse to avoid writing.

It's really very funny; after weeks and months of preparation, research, commitment, pain, toil, and trouble, after weeks of self-doubt, fears, and insecurities, after weeks of working your ass off, you may suddenly want to chuck it, with only a few pages to write.

It's absurd; you really can't take it too seriously.

What do you do?

What's happening is a common experience among writers. It originates below the level of awareness. Every writer I know, including myself, experiences this phenomenon. *Emotionally*, you don't want to end the screenplay. You want to hang on, not finish it. It's like a terrible relationship; no matter how bad it is, a terrible relationship is better than no relationship at all.

The same principle applies to writing your screenplay. It's hard to end. It's been a great part of your life; you think about it every day, your characters are like friends, you talk about your story every chance you get. Writing has kept you awake at night, caused you pain and suffering, given you great satisfaction. Of course you don't want to give it up!

For what?

It's only natural "to hold on."

I hate to spoil your illusions, but there's a lot of work left to do on this screenplay. When you finish this words-on-paper draft, you're only a third of the way through the screenwriting process. You're not done with anything; the ending of one thing is always the beginning of something else. You've got two more drafts to go before you complete this first-draft screenplay.

Just finish your script; resolve it. And once you write

"the end" give yourself a pat on the back and celebrate with a glass of wine, or champagne, or whatever else suits your disposition.

Put your screenplay on the desk in front of you and see how many pages you've written. Pick it up. Feel it.

You did it.

Then take a week off.

The hardest part of the screenwriting experience is complete. Now the work really begins.

The Exercise

Isolate the two or three dramatic elements of Act III that will resolve your story. Then structure Act III on fourteen 3 × 5 cards, the same as you did for Act I, and the first and second half of Act II.

When you feel comfortable with your material, start writing. If a new idea comes to you about a new screenplay, simply write it down.

If you experience any resistance, doubts, or judgments, just "bend with it," acknowledge it, and continue writing.

If you want to change the details of your ending, do it. If your ending comes out different from what you want it to be, write it one way, put it away in a drawer somewhere, and then write it again; this time it will be the way you want it. If you're writing a comedy and it comes out serious and dramatic, write it down, stick it in a drawer, and then write it as a comedy. The same with a drama; if it comes out funny, write it, stick it in a drawer somewhere and forget about it, then go back and write it the way you want to.

16

The Rewrite

Wherein we take what we've got and make it better:

One day while I was driving with a musician friend we saw a billboard showing a beautiful California blonde sunning herself at the beach; on the sidewalk below the billboard a young man was leading a little girl by the hand. It was a beautiful scene. As we drove by, my friend turned to me and muttered, "I am a child." It was a line for a song. He reached into the glove compartment, pulled out an old envelope, wrote down the line, added a few more words, hummed a musical phrase, and the whole song came to him. It took him only a few minutes to write down the lyrics.

When we got back to my house, he sat down at the piano and began to tie it together. About 10 minutes later he played the song for me. It sounded good, even though it was rough and sketchy.

A few days later he called and invited me to meet him at the recording studio. I went and heard the song performed by musicians backed by a large orchestra. I was blown away: from some scribbled lines on an old envelope to this intense musical experience! I couldn't believe it. I was jealous as hell; why couldn't I write a screenplay or a book like that! I left the studio filled with envy and self-pity. Oh, when I think of the days, the hours, the months, of arduous and tedious work that goes into writing a screenplay.

I would like to write a screenplay that way. But it's not to be.

The experience stayed with me and I didn't speak to my friend for several days. But suddenly I saw that the screenwriting experience is composed of many stages and they're all different. You may get a flash of inspiration for a script, but executing it is quite another story. It's a detailed, step-by-step process, and you move through it in stages, making it better and more complete as you go along.

It's only natural. Science teaches us that. The scientific method since the time of Bacon has involved experimentation; a scientist will try things, exploring each possible alternative, intelligently and systematically, keeping what works and discarding what doesn't.

Writing a screenplay is a *process*. Many people writing their first screenplay believe that all they have to do is write it, then have it typed up and sent out.

Nothing is further from the truth. Writing is a day-by-day job, three to five hours a day, five days a week, typing pages over and over again, cutting strips of paper and pasting them on the master pages. Rewriting your screenplay is necessary; it corrects the changes you've made during the first words-on-paper draft, then clarifies and defines your story and sharpens your characters and situations.

Writing a first-draft screenplay is done in three stages; first, the words-on-paper draft, which you've just finished; second, the "mechanical" stage, where you correct changes made during the writing, and third, the "polish" stage.

When you complete the first words-on-paper draft, you're ready to begin the second stage, the "mechanical" stage; you'll correct the changes you made during the first stage, bring the script to length, tighten up the dramatic tension, and sharpen the focus of your main character.

In this stage of the screenwriting process you're going to be changing things, a lot of things; you'll rewrite 80 percent of Act I, about 60 percent of the first half of Act II, about 25 percent of the second half of Act II, and about 10 or 15 percent of Act III.

Then you'll go into the third stage of the first draft, polishing, accenting, texturing each scene, changing a word here, a word there, a sentence here, a scene there, sometimes rewriting a scene some 10 or 15 times to make it right.

After you finish the first words-on-paper draft, and take a week to 10 days off, it's time to get back to work and begin the second stage of your screenplay. This rewrite of the first words-on-paper draft is the "mechanical" draft.

That's just what it is. Don't expect creative inspiration to guide you, because you're going to be correcting all those changes you made in the first and second act so your story line progresses from beginning to end. You've got to set it up properly, add new scenes that make it work, and delete those scenes that don't. You're going to be typing a lot in this draft, so be prepared for it.

The first thing you have to do is *see what you've got.* You probably don't know or remember what you did in the first act; when you're in the paradigm, you can't *see* the paradigm. You have no overview, no objective perspective about what you've done or not done.

The first thing you have to do is get an overview. The way to do that is read the entire first draft in one sitting from beginning to end. *Do not take notes* or write in the margins about the changes you want to make.

You might experience several emotional swings: "This is the worst thing I've ever read," is the most common response. "It's just awful, terrible." One student called me after she read her words-on-paper draft, screamed, "How could you let me write this?" and hung up. Later, I found out she threw her script down in total despair, crawled into bed, turned the electric blanket up to 9, maximum security, and assumed the prenatal position. She stayed this way for two days. She overreacted, of course, and sometimes reading what you've written can be a devastating experience. If it happens, just ride it out. I waited about four days before I called her back; I knew she was going to have to deal with all those "unreal" expectations she had. We talked about it and she said she didn't feel anything about it now, so I told her to just start rewriting Act I, and just do what she had to do to make it work. She did (she felt like a machine, she said) but believe it or not, it was some of her best writing. It took her about two weeks to regain her confidence and feel something toward her work. Your attitude should be simple: you know your script needs work, so you don't need anyone to tell you what you already know. How good or bad it is at this stage is absolutely irrelevant. What happens most of the time is that you get on a roller coaster; you'll like some of it, you'll hate some of it.

A rewrite is essential to make what you've written better. Accept it, don't argue with it, and don't fight it. That's just the way it is. Nobody ever told you writing a screenplay was going to be a piece of cake.

When you complete reading the words-on-paper draft, think about it. Make mental notes, nothing else. *Notice* what you have to do to set up those changes you made during Act II, and any other things you need to do to make the script work. Think about it a few hours, or better yet, let it cook overnight. You don't need to make any clearcut or defined decisions at this point.

You'll be working in 30-page units of action. You'll rewrite Act I, then the first half of Act II, then the second half of Act II, and then Act III.

You'll do most of the work in Act I. You're going to rewrite about 80 percent of this material.

Now read Act I and make extensive notes, either on the margin or on a pad. Any dialogue changes, scene changes, or shifts in action, plot, or character, will need to be integrated into the script as a whole.

When you know the changes you want to make, do new scene cards for Act I. Some scenes will be okay the way they are; some will not. Just take your 3 × 5 cards and lay them out for the new Act I. You'll probably need to write about five or six new scenes, change some of the dialogue in several scenes, and then polish, trim, and cut to length. This process should take about two weeks. Usually, Act I takes the longest time of the rewrite.

Rewriting the first act will be easier than you thought it would be. You've already established your writing discipline, and you know your story, so the execution of these changes should be easy and natural. Sometimes you might have difficulty deciding what to do, especially if Act I is too long. If that happens, you might need to transfer a few scenes from Act I to Act II.

Just do the rewrite for Act I. Work in 10-page units, and strive for clarity and simplicity of visual image. Tell your story, one scene at a time, one page at a time.

Concentrate on opening up your story visually. You'll

find in Act I you had a tendency to tell most of your story with dialogue. You'll "talk" your story. For example, your character may be driving a car and see a jewelry store. "I need a jade ring," your character says to her mother. "Let's stop." You end the scene and then cut to the next scene, where she shows off her new jade ring at a party.

This time *show* it; go *inside* the store, show your character standing at the counter buying the ring, then cut to the party scene.

Show your character walking in the park, jogging on the streets. Think visually; be aware of cinematic transitions, how you go from one scene into another; watch your lead ins and lead outs.

When you finish Act I, go back and clean it up a bit. Polish a scene or retype some pages, cut out a few lines of dialogue to make it clearer and tighter. Don't spend too much time on it; it's important to move forward through the screenplay; always work from beginning to end, beginning to end.

Move on to the first half of Act II. Read it and take notes on what you need to do to make it work. You'll find you'll be changing about 60 percent of the first half. Determine the changes you want to make, then lay out this section on 3 × 5 cards, just like Act I.

Know your dramatic context; make sure Pinch I is clean and tight and the midpoint clear and defined. If you need to do anything to make your story work, do it.

Tell your story visually. Try to cut down your dialogue scenes by focusing on the visual dynamics. Let Pinch I keep your story on track.

Does the midpoint still work effectively? Is it too long or too short? Do you need to redefine it visually?

Write the midpoint.

You'll spend a week or two on this section.

Move on to the second half of Act II. Read it through. Make notes on what you need to do to correct the changes. Structure the second half on fourteen 3 × 5 cards. Once you know what you need to do, execute it simply, keeping the dramatic context and time frame clearly in mind. You probably won't have to change more than 25–30 percent of the second half of Act II. Keep your story on track. Follow your main character through the development of your story; move forward through Pinch II and Plot Point II.

When you finished, don't spend too much time polishing this section because you'll spend a lot of time in doubt and confusion, and the creative urge might disappear. This section will only take you about a week to correct.

In Act III, you'll only need to rewrite about 10–15 percent of the words-on-paper draft. This will take you about a week. You might want to clean up and define your ending, refocus the resolution. The actual writing process itself at this time is clear-cut and simple to handle; you know exactly what you have to do to finish it.

If you have a large action sequence for your ending— like the destruction of the new Death Star in *Return of the Jedi*—you may want to draw a picture or "storyboard" what will happen.

When I was writing my first screenplay, an action-adventure story, I had an elaborate action scene for my ending. Six men creep into an enemy camp under cover of darkness, create a diversion, then rescue four friends who are being held prisoner. Think of the ending of *The Wild Bunch* or *The Professionals*. I had trouble writing the sequence, so I drew a picture of the location, then drew out the escape sequence; I found the way into the sequence and the way out of the sequence. Once I clearly knew what I wanted it to look like, I put the drawing away and wrote the sequence.

A screenplay is a story told in pictures, dialogue, and description. It didn't matter that I was making up a location; if the film was made, the script would be changed to fit the actual location site. Don't worry about whether the "exact" location exists; simply be clear about what you want to write, then write it. You should be able to finish this "mechanical" draft of your screenplay in about four to five weeks, and it should end up being anywhere from 110 to 120 pages, no longer. Your story line should be clear, with all the necessary changes fused into an organic story line from beginning to end.

You may or may not want to take a few days or a week off. Do what you want. You're ready to move into the third, or polish, stage of your first-draft screenplay.

This is where you'll really write your screenplay. You'll be typing a lot. The process of rewriting entails more typing than writing. You'll move three lines from a scene in Act I to another scene in the first half of Act II. You may type it up on a strip of paper and paste it on the page. You'll bridge one scene with another scene, and drop the transition; you'll telescope scenes; that is, you may take a scene from Act I, combine it with a scene in Act II, and end up with a scene shorter than either.

You'll accent, polish, hone, tighten, and texture your script; it's the most important stage of the screenwriting experience. You'll notice rhythm of action, you'll see places where a "pause," or a "beat" will strengthen the suspense of your scene. You'll reword; "he looks at the woman across from him," may become "he regards her questioningly." You'll sharpen visual images by adding adjectives, tighten and condense dialogue by cutting words from speeches, sometimes whole sentences, occasionally chunks of dialogue.

Again, work in 30-page units of action; do Act I, then the first half of Act II, then the second half of Act II, then Act III. Working in units like this allows you to control your story and move forward, step by step, toward the resolution.

Good structure, remember, is the relationship between the parts and the whole; it is like an ice cube and water, or fire and its heat. As you're polishing your screenplay, you'll subdue the structural elements until they are integral to the story.

Polish Act I. Read it, typing and cleaning it up as you move through scenes and pages. Cross out a sentence here, add a few words there, bridge this paragraph with this line of dialogue, and so on.

Tighten, trim, condense, polish, cut, cut, and cut some more. Most new writers don't like to cut words—or paragraphs—but you've got to be ruthless in this stage. If you're wondering whether you should keep this dialogue, paragraph, description, or scene, chances are you'll need to cut it.

The purpose of the polish stage is to make it the best screenplay you can.

How do you know when the rewrite's done? When can you lay down your pages and say "I've completed the first draft of my screenplay"? It's a difficult question. You never really know, but there are certain signs to look for. First of all, understand that your script will never be perfect. There will always be a few scenes that don't work. No matter how many times you write and rewrite, they'll never be right. You'll have to let those scenes go.

No one will ever notice they don't work or measure up to your expectations. It'll be easier to let go if you understand that.

You might find you're spending a lot of time on minor changes. (You'll change "but there are signs," to "and there are signs.") That's a sign that you're ready to stop.

Then let it go. It's going to stand or fall on its own. It's not going to be "perfect."

"Perfection is an ideal; it exists only in the mind, not in reality," Renoir said.

The Exercise

Read the words-on-paper draft; take no notes, just sit down and read it in one sitting. You'll make changes in your head as you're reading; other changes you'll deal with when you're actually writing pages.

Start with Act I. Read it as a unit of dramatic action and take notes, either in the margin or on a separate piece of paper. Structure and correlate any new scenes with the old scenes written, and then lay out Act I on fourteen 3 × 5 cards. When you're done, go over the cards until they feel comfortable, then begin writing. Your first few pages may be stilted and awkward; it's okay, don't worry about it.

Work in 30-page units, 10 pages at a time. You'll do between 10 and 15 pages a week. It will take you about two weeks to complete Act I.

Then move into the first half of Act II. Read it, take notes, then structure it on 3 × 5 cards.

Start rewriting, one scene at a time, one page at a time,

through Pinch I to midpoint. Be clear on your dramatic context.

Write the midpoint, and be sure that the focus of your story is clear and defined; then move into the second half of Act II. Use the same process; read the unit, take notes, structure on 3 × 5 cards, then start writing.

The same with Act III. Bring it to length, and make all the changes needed for a consistent story line.

When you've completed the "mechanical" stage of the first-draft screenplay, move into the "polish" stage. Again, work in 30-page units of dramatic action; polish, hone, clean, tighten, accent, cut, and shade your material.

Your name is on the title page, so do the best job you can.

Remember, a screenplay is a reading experience before it becomes a visual experience.

17

The "Good Read"

Wherein we discuss the search for the "good read":

During my two years as head of the story department at Cinemobile Systems and Cine Artists, I read more than 2,000 screenplays and at least 100 novels in my search for material. I found only 40 screenplays worth submitting to our financial partners. In spite of my acquired cynicism, I picked up every new screenplay with the hope that this one was going to knock me on my ass. I wanted that to happen, badly. Talk to any reader in Hollywood and he or she will tell you the same thing.

I was always looking for the "good read."

What is a "good read"? I never knew how to define it exactly; I could only say it "looked" a certain way, and "read" a certain way, and "felt" a certain way. A good screenplay works from page one, paragraph one, word one. *Chinatown* was a good read; so was *Body Heat, Absence of Malice*, and *Annie Hall.*

There's a lot of space on the page, the descriptive paragraphs are short and to the point, and the dialogue moves along from scene to scene with interest and suspense. The reader keeps turning the pages.

That is the writer's job: to keep the reader turning pages.

What does the reader look for?

Story, character, and style, first and foremost. The first thing that attracts me is the writing style, the way the words are put down on paper: lean, tight, crisp, and visual. Then the premise. Does it grab my attention? Is it interesting? How is the script set up in terms of story, and visual dynamics? Are the characters well-rounded and three-dimensional? Is there enough information presented during the first ten pages to make me want to continue reading?

When you find a "good read," you know it; there's a certain excitement and energy on the first page. People hate to read in Hollywood, yet everybody loves to read a good screenplay. Things never change in that respect.

As an example, I thought it would be interesting to include a reader's evaluation sheet from a major film company. It will show you where the reader is coming from.

First, in the left-hand corner of the page, there is the *genre*, a one-word description of the type of story: action-adventure, love story, western, comedy, romantic comedy, farce, romance, sad or happy ending, science fiction, animated, or futuristic. In this case the genre *romance, with sad ending*.

Second, there is a brief synopsis of the story, a four- or five-line description of *what* the story is about; in this example the synopsis reads: "A beautiful, ambitious young attorney schemes to get ahead in a Chicago-based law firm. Her boss, married with three kids, falls in love with her. She subtly demands to be made a full partner, which ruins him politically. His marriage on the rocks, he leaves to start his own firm, making her the sole partner. Within weeks, he's begging his wife to take him back. Our girl steams ahead.''

That's what the story is about; the subject of the screenplay. (If you want to read good synopses, read any movie description in *TV Guide*. That's the way you've got to tell *your* story before you even write it.)

Third, after this brief synopsis, there is a one-and-a-half page detailed summary of the story, in depth and detail, which I have omitted.

Fourth, there is a reader's *analysis*, with structure and character emphasized. In this particular evaluation, the analysis is broken down like this (sometimes, it includes a chart, with boxes in which to check excellent, good, fair, or poor for character, dialogue, and structure):

I—Character

  A) Design: A ruthless young career woman takes advantage of a middle-aged husband and father, and he abandons his family for her.

  B) Development: Almost good. The author must have it in for women. This is one of the bitchiest portrayals since *Darling* or *Petulia*. The characters just don't ring true. They're not full enough.

II—Dialogue

  Fair. This is Chicago but it's very small time. The dialogue here makes the cardinal sin of making *everything* obvious. The story is told in dialogue.

III—Structure

A) Design:	A Lolita with brains works her way up the ladder in the legal world by manipulating her boss, a family man, and then dumping him once she's accomplished her primary goals.
B) Development:	Fair. Because it's all so obvious and soap opera oriented. The main character has no depth, she's too much an unsympathetic character.
C) Pacing:	Good. Though there's no doubt about what's going to happen next, and very little dramatic tension. But it doesn't drag either.
D) Resolution:	Poor. The script suddenly ends. We are left up in the air. The poor husband goes crawling home and we never see the main character again.

That's the analysis and breakdown of structure and character. Then there is a *Reader's recommendation*, where the reader adds his or her impressions in a few sentences: "Not recommended. A mediocre romantic drama in every respect. It's the unsympathetic portrait of a pushy, midwestern career woman. The ultimate point of the whole thing remains a mystery. It's downbeat, but totally without the black comedy textures one associates with Nabokov, or others of the ilk. Cornbelt soap opera, not a feature film."

That is a Hollywood reader's synopsis of a screenplay. And as short and curt as it is, it is what every studio executive and agent and movie producer reads.

What's the reader going to say about your screenplay?

As an exercise you might want to familiarize yourself

with this evaluation. This is where the reader comes from. From his or her point of view there's always another script to read; usually the pile on the desk is about two feet high. Everybody's writing screenplays, and when the readers read the scripts, 99 times out of 100 they are disappointed.

This year more than 18,000 screenplays and teleplays will be registered at the Writer's Guild of America–West. Out of all these, less than 80 films will be made in Hollywood.

Despite this, the eighties will be remembered as the decade of the screenwriter. More people are writing screenplays than ever before. And within the next few years, the number of people writing for the film medium—film, TV, cable, and disc—will double and triple in size.

We have evolved into a visual society; less than 30 years ago, we were still essentially a literary society. That changed with the growth of television, and is now changing again as we move into the age of the computer. We are in the midst of an information revolution. Children grow up playing video games, they learn how to program in grade school.

The marketplace for the screenwriter is changing; within this decade the need for film writers will explode. The vast spectrum of cable will stabilize, and companies will soon be producing specialized material. The entire motion picture and television market will be something other than what it is today. No one knows exactly *what* this market will be, but one thing is certain: the opportunities for the screenwriter will be enormous.

If you're serious about writing a screenplay, now is the time to sharpen your skills and perfect your craft.

The future is *now*.

A lot of people tell me they want to write screenplays.

They call me, write me, badger me, finally join a workshop, and then two or three weeks later drop out without a word. Their commitment, to themselves and to their writing, was zero. Action *is* character; what a person does is what he is, not what he says.

If you're going to do it, do it.

That's what this book is about. It is a guide and a tool. You may read this book a hundred times, but until you put it down and do the exercises, you're only going to be *thinking* about writing a screenplay and not writing one.

It takes time, patience, effort, and commitment to write a screenplay. Are you willing to make that commitment to yourself? Are you willing to learn and make mistakes? Are you willing to do the best job you can?

What's really important about writing a screenplay is doing it. You set yourself a goal, a task, and you achieve it. That's what it's all about.

When people complete their first-draft screenplay in my workshops, everybody applauds; it is our acknowledgment of the time and the work and the toil and the effort and the pain and the joy that went into the writing.

The Screenwriter's Workbook will guide you through the screenwriting process. The more you put in, the more you're going to get out. That's just a natural law.

"True art," Jean Renoir told me, "is in the *doing* of it."

Writing is a personal responsibility; either you do it, or you don't.

Do it.

Index